Chil

AND

Spirit

Also by Linda Williamson

Mediums and Their Work
Contacting the Spirit World
Mediums and the Afterlife

Acknowledgements

The author wishes to thank the following
for permission to quote from their books:
June Cowlin – *Truth is Veiled* and *Listen Who Dares*;
Headline – Peter Fenwick, *The Truth in the Light*;
Sobel Weber Associates/Bantam Books – Raymond Moody,
The Light Beyond; Pan Books – Harold S. Kushner,
When Bad Things Happen to Good People;
Sparrowhawk Press – Carol E. Parrish-Harra,
The New Age Handbook on Death and Dying.

CONTENTS

I would like to thank all those who helped me in the compilation of this book, particularly the bereaved parents who have shared their stories with me, reliving many painful memories in the process. This book is dedicated to them and to their children who have proved from the spirit world that death is the gateway to life.

God's Lent Child

I'll lend you for a little while
A child of mine, God said –
For you to love the while he lives,
And mourn for when he's dead.
It may be six or seven years
Or forty two or three,
But will you, till I call him back,
Take care of him for me?

He'll bring charms to gladden you
And (should his stay be brief)
You'll have his memories
As a solace for your grief.
I cannot promise he will stay
Since all from earth return
But there are lessons taught below
I want this child to learn.

I've looked this whole world over
In my search for teachers true,
And from the things that crowd life's lanes
I have chosen you.
Now will you give him all your love
Nor think the labour vain?
Nor hate me when I come to take
This lent child back again?

I fancied that I heard them say,
'Dear Lord, Thy will be done,
For all the joys thy child will bring
The risk of grief we'll run.
We will shelter him with tenderness
We'll love him while we may
And for the happiness we've known
Forever grateful stay.

But should Thy Angels call for him
Much sooner than we've planned
We'll brave the bitter grief that comes
And try to understand.'

Anon

INTRODUCTION

Margaret was unable to hold back the tears as she spoke to me. 'Why us?' she demanded. 'Why our son? What have we done to deserve this?'

Her husband John, who was sitting beside her, reached out and squeezed her hand. A reserved man, his face showed little emotion but I could hear the pain and anger in his voice.

'David was a good boy. He was never any trouble. If there is a God, why does he allow these things to happen?'

Their son David, who was sixteen, had been to visit friends and was riding home on his bicycle when a car came out of a side turning and collided with him. He was thrown off and sustained horrific head injuries as he was dragged under the wheels of the vehicle. The driver of the car called an ambulance but David was dead by the time it got there. That had been a month before. His shocked and devastated parents had come to me, as a medium, in the hope that I could make contact with him and reassure them that he was all right.

'It may sound silly,' Margaret confided. 'I'm not psychic or anything but ever since he died I've felt him around me. The other day I was standing at the sink doing the washing-up and I could have sworn he was standing behind me but when I turned round there was no one there.'

'I've felt him too,' John admitted. 'At least, I'd like to think so but I'm probably just imagining it because I want it to be true.'

'He *is* with you,' I assured them. 'I can sense him here now.' And I described his personality as I sensed his spirit presence: his humour, his thoughtfulness and the habit he had of brushing the hair out of his eyes.

'That's it exactly,' Margaret exclaimed as I made the gesture that had been so characteristic of David.

'Can you see him?' John asked.

I had to explain that I don't as a rule see the spirit people who come through when I am giving a consultation, or sitting, as it is called. It is more of a mental picture or impression. But I described the image I had in my mind.

'He was tall and slim with fairish hair, quite long.'

His father smiled. 'That's right. I was always on at him to get it cut.'

'He's talking about his sister,' I went on, hearing David's voice inside my head. 'She's younger than him.'

'Yes,' Margaret agreed. 'They were very close.'

'He wants you to pass on his love to her.'

'I'll do that. She'll be so pleased to hear from him.'

'He's telling me the accident happened on a long, straight stretch of road. It wasn't far from where he lived. He says it wasn't his fault. He was going quite slowly and wearing a crash helmet. The driver turned out without looking.'

They confirmed that this was true. I went on, relaying all the words and impressions David was putting into my mind, not only about the accident but about other things in his life. I knew he was making a great effort to get through to me and I wanted to give his parents the conviction that he really was there in the room with us.

'Is he happy?' Margaret asked anxiously.

'Yes,' I told her without hesitation. I wished I could find words to convey adequately the emotions I was picking up, the immense love he had for his parents and the sense of joy and freedom that those in the spirit world bring with them. 'He's in no pain. He left that behind with his physical body. He's strong now and he's going to give you the strength to get through this.'

'We're not disturbing him,' she wanted to know, 'by trying to get in touch with him?'

I promised her that she wasn't. In fact, she was helping him by giving him the opportunity to communicate. When people die they are able to come back and see those they have left behind. It distresses them to see them grieving and they long to be able to say, as David did, 'Don't worry about me. I'm all right.'

John shook his head. 'I accept what you're saying but it still doesn't make any sense to me. A young life, just snuffed out like that . . . What's the point?'

'Your son is telling me that there is a reason. He doesn't fully understand it himself yet but he's been told by some-one who is looking after him there that the accident was part of a plan. He had achieved what he came to earth to do. It was time to move on.'

'But he had his whole life in front of him,' John protested.

I understood John's reaction but I explained how I saw it. Having received communication from so many young people and studied the words of spiritual teachers in this world and the next, I do believe that we, in this life, have a very limited view of the plan of destiny that is being worked out for each one of us. We are all immortal souls. Whether we live on this earth for nine years or ninety years, it is still only an infinitesimal part of our existence. We come to earth for a purpose and sometimes a short life is all that is needed. In human terms, death is a tragedy but in spiritual terms it is the beginning of a new life on a higher plane of being.

I could see that John and Margaret were puzzled by what I was trying to put across. At present, understandably, all they could think about was how much they missed their son. But I hoped that in time, when the impact of their grief lessened, they would explore these ideas for themselves and find a way of making sense of what had happened. In the meantime, I was glad that I had been able to give them some comfort, something that would help them cope in the dark days that lay ahead.

We talked for a long time. When they left, they were looking a little brighter.

'I feel better,' Margaret said, 'knowing he's all right.'

'You've given us a lot to think about.' John shook my hand. 'If he's happy I suppose I shouldn't wish him back but, all the same . . . there's nothing I wouldn't give to have him back with us again.'

Parents' Grief

John's parting words went straight to my heart. I have heard them echoed by so many bereaved parents. I feel deeply for those who suffer in this way, for it is the most devastating loss any parent can be called upon to face. The death of an elderly person, such as a mother, father or grandparent is sad, but at least there is the consolation of knowing that they have had a full life. In the case of a child there is a terrible sense of waste; a young life, snatched away before its time. It seems a violation of the natural order. Parents don't expect their children to die before them.

Each death brings its own particular kind of sorrow.

There is the sudden shock of losing a son or daughter in an accident or the lingering torture of watching a child die slowly and painfully through disease. Who can say which is worse? Then there are the handicapped children who, in their innocent and trusting way, bring so much love to those around them, and the troubled ones who take their own lives, leaving their parents full of unresolved guilt and questions that may never be answered.

The death of a baby brings perhaps the greatest sense of futility and pointless suffering. These little ones are deprived of the chance to experience life and their parents are denied the joy of watching them grow up. But age makes no difference and adult children are missed just as sorely as young ones, often with added anxiety about the families they in their turn may have left behind.

A ninety-year-old woman whose sixty-five-year-old daughter died of cancer confided to me sadly, 'She was still my little girl and now she's gone, my life is so empty. I wish I could have died instead of her.'

Nor should it be thought that parents are the only ones to suffer; much of what I say about parents could equally apply to other relatives. For the death of a child shatters the whole family. Grandparents, uncles, aunts and friends all suffer the loss, as do brothers and sisters. And they may feel neglected and unloved if their parents are so wrapped up in their own grief that they don't notice how much the siblings are missing the one who has gone.

Parents who are committed Christians can at least draw comfort from the belief that their child is in heaven and at peace but the majority of people don't have that sort of unquestioning faith. They may have been brought up in the belief that we go to heaven when we die but this Sunday School philosophy no longer holds any meaning for them. Some have never had any religious belief. For them, death is the end of existence; a dark void. But there are many who do have an intuitive awareness that there must be something beyond, something that makes sense of this life, with all its suffering, though they cannot imagine what any sort of Afterlife could be like.

In this respect, John and Margaret were typical of my sitters. John had always considered himself an agnostic. Margaret had been brought up a Roman Catholic, though she no longer went to church. Neither of them would previously have dreamed of going to see a medium. As John said, 'We thought mediums were weird until we met you!'

I took that as a compliment. I was glad to know I had removed some of their misconceptions. As they discovered, I don't sit in a dark room holding hands round a seance table, nor do I wear beads or gaze into a crystal ball. My job is to act as a messenger for those who have passed into the world of spirit. I do this by attuning my mind to them and passing on whatever they want to say.

It doesn't look very dramatic. And sometimes it is not possible to establish contact with the person the sitter wants to hear from. But I do know, after twenty years of doing this work, that spirit communication is a fact and that those in the next world can and do come back to those on earth, bringing them love and comfort.

The Purpose of This Book

In this book I have told the stories of parents who have found this comfort for themselves, through the evidence they have received from mediums. I have also written about that sense of their children's presence that is often experienced, even by people who think they are devoid of any psychic ability, and which is not imagination but is their child's love reaching out to them. And I have tried to offer some answers to the apparently unanswerable question – why do innocent children have to suffer and die?

I have written, too, of children's feelings about death. Children are closer to the spirit world than adults and sometimes have a spiritual perception that their parents might envy. Indeed, many young children, as this book shows, have natural psychic ability. Adults can learn much from children, if only they will listen to them and treat their insights with the seriousness they deserve.

There is also much to be learned from the near-death experiences of children. Those little ones who have been to the brink of death and have been saved by doctors have spoken of entering a beautiful world beyond, where there was no more pain but peace, joy and love.

I have not dwelt too much in this book upon the pain of losing a child. Any parent who has been bereaved knows what it is like and they don't need me to tell them. Nor have I dwelt upon the details of the children's deaths, the illnesses and the accidents, since this would only stir up dreadful memories for anyone whose own child had died in the same way. Instead, I have concentrated upon the help parents have found and the strength this has given them to take up their own lives again. For I never cease to be amazed at the resilience of the parents I meet, their courage in overcoming terrible suffering and their determination to bring out of it something positive that will help others. And I would like to pass on to anyone in this situation a message of hope, summed up in the words of the poet Rabindranath Tagore: 'Death is not extinguishing the light; it is putting out the lamp because the dawn has come.'

Note: For the sake of convenience, I have sometimes used the word 'he' when referring to a child, though, of course, everything I say applies equally to boys and girls.

1

WHEN A CHILD DIES

In the course of my work I have met many parents in different stages of grief. Some have only recently lost their child and are in that first state of shock, where the realisation of what has happened has not quite sunk in. Others have had time to come to terms with the tragedy but the sadness is still with them. As any parent knows who has been through this trauma, the death of a child is not something you get over. Some mothers whose children died ten, twenty or even thirty years ago have still burst into tears when talking to me about them. Time, as one mother said to me, doesn't so much heal the wounds as paper over the cracks. You learn to adjust to the loss and to get on with your life with at least a semblance of normality.

To lose a child is to lose not only your delight in their company but also your hopes for the future: watching them grow up, wondering what they will do with their lives, whether they will have children of their own. You may have other much-loved children but they cannot replace the one who has been taken away, nor can anything fill the gap that is left in your heart and mind. A part of your own being has gone and life can never be the same again.

One thing I never say to bereaved parents is, 'I know

how you feel'. I can use my imagination to put myself in
their place and I understand something of what they are
going through because I have listened to so many parents
describing their feelings. But I cannot actually know because
I have never lost a child myself. In fact, no one can truly
understand the agony a child's death causes unless they have
been through it themselves. Those who have are bound
together by a shared grief. As one mother commented, 'It's
like belonging to a very exclusive club of which no one
wants to be a member.'

Parents feel very isolated at these times. They need
someone to talk to, so that they can give vent to all the
pain, anger and guilt they are feeling. They need a shoul-
der to cry on, when tears are the only thing that brings
relief. But often they don't get this kind of support. In
fact, they find that friends tend to avoid them; not out of
callousness, though it may seem like that, but because they
don't know how to offer comfort. Death is a taboo subject
in our society. People don't know what to say. They feel
awkward, embarrassed, especially when it is a child who
has died.

'I felt as though I'd suddenly become invisible,' one
mother, Jacky, confided to me. 'Even some of my oldest
friends would cross the road to avoid speaking to me. It was
as though I had a contagious disease they were afraid of
catching.'

Sensing this embarrassment, parents try to put a
brave face on things, pretending they are coping when
inwardly they are falling apart. Well-meaning remarks,
such as 'you'll feel better in time' or 'at least you still have
the other children', are at best unhelpful, at worst deeply
wounding. Nor do you want people trying to cheer you up
and 'take your mind off things'. Most parents, mothers
especially, want to talk and talk about their children
and to cry. Fathers are more reluctant to express their

emotions and need to be encouraged to get their feelings out into the open rather than suppressing them. The most helpful friends are the ones who are prepared just to be there and just to listen, with kindness, sympathy and endless patience.

The Grieving Process

Grieving takes time and it is a process that cannot be hurried. A mother who was told, a year after her baby's death, 'you should be over that by now', admitted that she felt like hitting the person who made that thoughtless remark. The first year after the bereavement is usually the worst, but the pain can resurface, sometimes years afterwards, in unexpected bouts of intense emotion.

Grief is a very personal thing. Everyone has to find their own way of coping with it. Some hide their suffering behind a false mask of cheerfulness, refusing to acknowledge their feelings, even to themselves. Others throw themselves into frantic activity, hoping that, if they keep busy, they won't have time to think.

The array of emotions thrown up by the grieving process can be bewildering. Periods of depression, when life does not seem worth living, alternate with periods of numbness, when all feeling seems to be suspended, or with times of restlessness and hyperactivity. Exhaustion is a common reaction. Even getting up in the morning takes an almost superhuman effort. There may be erratic mood swings and outbursts of anger and irritability, even with those you love who are trying to help you.

All this can impose an intolerable strain on family life. Some couples are brought closer together but others are driven apart. The partners are so weighed down by their

individual grief that they do not have the strength to support each other. Resentment may arise if they have different ways of trying to cope. For instance, the man may
seek consolation in his work and spend most of his time
out of the house, leaving his wife feeling abandoned and
alone. She in turn may retreat into herself, shutting her
partner out emotionally and rejecting his attempts to comfort her. I have seen many marriages break down through
such misunderstandings, causing further distress to those
involved.

Seeing Other Children

One of the hardest things for parents who have lost a child is
to watch other parents with their children. Valerie, whose
son Mark was the victim of a car accident (so many young
people die in this way), spoke to me of her feelings, more
than a year after his death:

> Wherever you go, you see smiling, happy faces and
> you think, they are normal, they have a normal life.
> And you want to grab hold of them and tell them,
> 'I've lost my son!' It's like being in a deep dark well.
> You can hear the joking and the laughter up above
> you and you are at the bottom.

If the child was living at home, the house now seems so
quiet and empty.

'I was always complaining about his loud music and
telling him to tidy up his room,' Valerie said. 'Now I'd
give anything to have that noise and untidiness back
again.'

The first anniversaries, Christmases and birthdays are
ordeals which parents dread. No smiling, excited faces, no
presents to be opened. Visiting places you associated with

your child, or where you used to go together, is equally difficult.

Valerie admitted that she could no longer go into the supermarket where Mark used to work on Saturdays. 'I used to see the boys at the tills in their brown uniforms and, without my glasses, I could easily imagine that one of them could be Mark.'

To go into a child's room, to see their photo or handle their belongings, is intolerably painful. Some parents are never able to clear out their child's room. It remains exactly as they left it, a sad shrine to their memory.

Parents look back with bitter regret to times when they denied the child something he or she wanted, even though they may have refused for their own good. All the little arguments and upsets of the past flood back into their minds. Who hasn't told a child off for being naughty or got impatient with them when they wouldn't do as they were told? When, suddenly, they are taken away by death, these small incidents get magnified out of all proportion.

Some parents torment themselves with guilt, blaming themselves for what happened. 'If only I hadn't let her go out that night . . .' 'If only I hadn't given him that bicycle for his birthday.' 'If only I'd told him how much I loved him . . .' There are so many 'If onlys', so many recriminations. The thoughts go round and round, an incessant torment. But it is too late to turn back the clock.

Life After Death and Spiritualism

It is the finality of death that seems so terrible; to think that you will never see your child again, never hear their voice or be able to give them a hug. But death is not final. This, as a medium, is what I try to help people to understand. When someone dies, they simply leave the body behind like an empty shell; their mind and personality live on unchanged. And the world we enter at death is not far removed from this world; they can still come back to us.

I know that this is difficult for many parents to believe. For most of them, it is the first time that they have been confronted with the death of someone they love. Often they remark to me, 'I never thought about death before. I never had to.' Now they are being forced to think about it in the cruellest way. And so they start to ask themselves whether there might, just possibly, be something beyond but they don't know how to begin to find out. They have never been to church. They are afraid to raise the subject of the Afterlife with friends or relatives in case they are thought odd.

Yet there is nothing odd in believing in life after death. From ancient times, man has always been instinctively aware that we live beyond the grave, and all the major religions enshrine this teaching. The Eastern religions claim that we return to earth many times in different incarnations. Christianity denies this, yet the belief that Jesus rose from the dead and appeared to His disciples lies at the heart of the Christian creed. It is only our modern Western world that has rejected all this ancient knowledge in favour of the scientific world view. According to this so-called 'rational' view, only things we can see, hear or touch are real; whereas everything spiritual is dismissed as hallucination or delusion.

Yet, even in the West, things are changing. Church attendance may be declining but people everywhere are waking up to the idea that there is more to life than the physical, material world. It is becoming more acceptable to talk about life after death. In fact, these days I seldom meet anyone who has a completely closed mind on the subject.

Spiritualism has done much to bring about this shift in public opinion. The Spiritualist movement began in America in the 1840s and is now a well-established religion, with

churches and centres all over the world. Its main teaching
is that we survive death and live on in the spiritual dimension and it seeks to demonstrate this through the work of
mediums, who have the gift of communicating with the
next world. Over the last hundred years and more,
parapsychologists have investigated the mediums' claims.
In many cases they have found that, contrary to their
expectations, mediums have been able to provide proof, by
describing spirit communicators and giving information
about them that they could not possibly have obtained in
any other way. Numerous books have been written about
this, and anyone who studies this subject with an open mind
is forced to conclude that the weight of evidence in favour
of survival is almost overwhelming.

Today, Spiritualism continues to provide this evidence,
but unfortunately the majority of people don't know about
it. Mediums have a bad reputation. They are thought of as
little old ladies conducting seances in back parlours. I find
this sad, because it means that many people who could
benefit so much from what Spiritualism has to offer don't
think to investigate it. Those who do consult mediums
find, to their surprise, how wrong the popular impressions
are. For one thing, mediums are not all women, elderly or
otherwise; nor do they sit in dark rooms calling up spirits.
Spiritualism is a very practical religion. It accepts that
people who have been bereaved need verifiable proof that
those they love are with them, and a plausible explanation
of what happens when we die, and mediums do their best to
provide this.

Some parents who are churchgoers are worried that
they shouldn't be consulting a medium, because their
church tells them it is wrong to 'dabble in the occult'. They
come to me looking slightly furtive, saying things like,
'I daren't tell the vicar I've been to see you!' This attitude
on the part of the Church puts sincere believers in a very

difficult position. They may sense that their children are near and be desperate to make contact with them, yet they are afraid that, in doing so, they will be committing a sin in the eyes of God.

Fortunately, many churchmen today are becoming more open-minded. There is nothing sinful in loving communication with those on the other side of life. Mediums do not deal with evil spirits, nor do they 'call up the dead'. They speak with deceased relatives, friends and teachers who come to give comfort and guidance and they seek to serve God in their own way by proving that death does not separate us from those we love.

I believe that this proof is the greatest consolation that can be offered to any parent. Of course, it doesn't take away the pain of loss or stop them from wishing that their child was still with them. They would hardly be human if they didn't miss their presence. But, if they understand that their child's existence is not at an end, and that they are still close, it does help to relieve the terrible sense of emptiness and despair.

Arranging the Funeral

Arranging and attending the funeral, although this is a heart-breaking task, is also made a little easier if parents realise that death is not the end. It is only the physical remains that are being buried or – scattered to the wind in the form of ashes. The child's essence – their mind, their personality – lives on.

Some parents like to plan the service with great care, choosing appropriate readings and perhaps including some of the child's favourite music. It may sound macabre to talk of a person attending their own funeral, but your child will probably be there in spirit, drawn close by the thoughts and prayers that are being sent out to them.

The decision as to whether to have a burial or a cremation can be a hard one to make. This really makes no difference to the child. They cannot be hurt in any way by what happens to the empty shell they have left behind. Nor will they be harmed if their organs are donated. In fact, they will probably be glad to know that they have been able to help someone else in this way.

Viewed from the spirit world, death is the start of a new existence. Inevitably, there are tears on our side of life but a funeral can also be an opportunity for the family and friends to come together and celebrate the child's life, and to wish them God speed as they embark on their journey.

Premonitions of Death

Even in cases where a child has been ill for some time, the death, when it comes, is a terrible shock to the parents. Their initial reaction is disbelief. 'This can't be happening – not my child, not me!' Yet, in talking to mothers, I have been struck by how many of them had some premonition of what was to come and knew, in their heart of hearts, that their child was not destined to be with them for long.

The mother's premonition may take the form of an inner knowledge that is with her from the time her child is born, or even before. Astrid Simensen, who lives in Sweden, told me:

> When my son Patrick was born I had a mental
> picture of an accident. I told my husband about it.
> We were both very protective of him, although we
> tried not to be over-protective. For instance, we

wouldn't allow him to have a motorbike when he
wanted one. I think we both knew subconsciously
that he wouldn't stay long.

When Patrick was in his teens, Astrid had another, more
urgent prompting:

It was Christmas Eve. We were all together, my
ex-husband, my other son Stephan and me. We were
very merry. But I felt very sad all of a sudden, I
didn't know why. The tears just started. Patrick came
over and held me and I had to tell him I didn't know
why I was crying. Was I being warned? He lived with
his father in Oslo, so it was the last time he was in
my home.

Then, towards the end of January, I felt compelled
to go to Oslo. There was no reason for me to go, as I
had seen Patrick just three weeks before, but the
thought would not leave me. I met Patrick and we
went out for a meal together, just him and me. We
talked about how nice it was to be together. The next
morning I went back to Stockholm.

That night I was very restless. I kept tossing and
turning in my sleep. My husband had an
appointment with the dentist the following morning
and I insisted on going with him. He wanted me to
stay in bed and rest for a while but I couldn't. I felt
very nervous and didn't want to be left in the house
on my own. (I have never before been afraid of
staying alone in the house.) I was troubled but I
didn't know why. Fifteen minutes after we got home
from the dentist's, the police came to tell me about
the accident. Patrick had gone the night before to a
school reunion in Oslo. With some friends, he had
gone to the top of the building to look at the stars.

He had fallen down a ventilation shaft that wasn't marked. He had just turned seventeen.

Lorraine, from South London, was given a warning in a vivid dream:

> I dreamed that a couple of policemen came to the door and told me that Wayne had been killed in an accident riding his motorbike. I didn't tell anyone about it and tried to put it out of my mind. Then, one night, two months later there was a knock at the door. When I opened it there were two policemen standing there. My heart sank.

The policemen gave her the news she dreaded: Wayne had been knocked off his motorbike by a driver who hadn't even bothered to stop.

A Mother's Intuition

It is nearly always mothers who have these premonitions – you could call it female intuition. Women seem to be more psychic by nature than men, though this may be because men are suspicious of anything irrational and don't listen to their own inner promptings. But there is undoubtedly a psychic link between mothers and their children. As one mother explained to me, 'Your marriage partner, however close you are to them, is still a separate person. Your children, because you have carried them inside you, are part of you. Even when they grow up, they are still emotionally inside you.'

A mother may instinctively sense when her child is ill, and will worry even if there are no outward signs of illness or the doctors tell her there is nothing amiss. She may know when her child is coming home and have a meal ready on the table. The same instinct will warn her when her child is in danger or dying, even though they may be separated by hundreds of miles.

Jacky was on holiday with her husband in Spain, when she woke up early one morning with terrible pains in her legs.

'I feel as if I have been run over by a steamroller,' she remarked to her husband.

She had no idea what could have caused her to be in such agony. Later that morning, they received a phone call from England. Their son Mark had been knocked down by a car at the same time that she had felt the pains.

This special bond that exists between mothers and their children does not end with death. When a child dies, the mother often feels that he or she is still with her. In fact, this experience is so common that I would say it is unusual for a mother not to have some sense of her child's presence, however vague or faint it may be. The same telepathy, or mind-to-mind contact, still exists, even though they are in different dimensions.

The awareness can take many different forms. It may be a vision, a dream, a voice speaking inside your mind. Or there may be just a feeling that they are in the room with you. Margaret's impression of her son standing behind her while she was doing the washing-up is very typical.

Georgiana Monckton describes a similar feeling in her book *Dear Isobel*, about her baby daughter who died of a brain tumour. One evening, a few weeks after Isobel had died, Georgiana went into her room:

> I sat in her rocking chair and looked into her cot.
> What was usually a rather empty, cold room,
> suddenly became full of warmth, full of Isobel. I
> wasn't consciously aware of Isobel being there, I just
> felt warm inside, comfortable and reassured. It was
> just like being in Isobel's room when she was alive. I

felt really peaceful and at ease with life. I must have sat there for five or more minutes. I got up, touched her cot and walked out. I remember thinking to myself that it felt so comforting I would do it again the following evening.

The next day I went into Isobel's room, sat down in her rocking chair – and burst out crying. She wasn't there. It was then I realised that perhaps she'd been in the room the day before. The difference was unbelievable. It was back to the cold, empty room that hadn't been helpful. It was extraordinary. I couldn't have imagined the difference in feeling, in temperature, in atmosphere. I really believe it was Isobel's way of saying, 'Mummy, I'm alright, I'm with you.'

The sense of presence often comes when you least expect it. It slips into the mind easily and effortlessly, perhaps when you are in the middle of some everyday task or in that dreamy state between waking and sleeping. It brings a comfort that warms the heart and lifts, if only for a few moments, the heavy weight of grief.

Lynne Heston told me:

I was in the garden hanging out the washing. It was the day before my son Martin's funeral. I had a sudden impression that he was very happy, much happier than when he had been on the earth plane. That feeling was very strong. I was so overwhelmed with it, after all the terrible sadness we had been going through and, of course, not looking forward to the funeral the next day. But this experience gave me a lot of strength.

I have heard this contact described in so many ways – 'a surge of energy', 'an inner glow', 'a peace that comes from nowhere, just when you're at your lowest ebb'. Mothers may not feel able to confide in anyone about these feelings for fear that even their families will not understand. Fathers who have such experiences – and many do – feel even less able to talk about them. Men are not supposed to be illogical!

The Sense of Presence

Parents who have this sense that their child is still close to them often wonder if they are imagining it. They are afraid of deluding themselves because they so want it to be true. If they talk to outsiders about it – and most of them are understandably reluctant to mention it – they are told, very kindly, that it is all in the mind. Doctors are seldom helpful, as most of them regard psychic experiences as signs of mental disorder. Bereavement counsellors accept that parents do have these feelings. They are forced to do so because they are so common. But they write them off as part of the grieving process and seldom attribute any validity to them.

Support groups tend to be a little more open but are equally wary of anything psychic. For instance, members of the Society of Compassionate Friends (see Useful Addresses), the biggest support group in the country for bereaved parents, have told me that, while they found the companionship of other parents comforting, they felt discouraged from discussing life after death or mentioning any contact they had had with their children. It should be said, however, that some branches of the Society are more receptive to the idea than others and that the Society's postal lending library does carry a range of books on the Afterlife.

The sceptical attitude they encounter all around them leaves parents not knowing what to think. As they are in such a vulnerable state, they can easily be persuaded that they are having hallucinations and begin to doubt their own sanity. So, if you are in this situation, how can you tell whether it is imagination or not?

This is where you have to trust your own intuition rather than being swayed by others. It is true that the mind can play tricks and it is possible to imagine that your child is there when they are not, especially if you are missing them and longing for them. But you are on the inside and only you know what you are feeling, so listen to the inner voice and trust what your heart tells you. If you sense that your child is there, then in all probability they are there, and are doing their best to let you know about it!

At least give yourself, and them, the benefit of the doubt. Think how frustrating it must be for them if, every time they succeed in making some impression upon your mind, you dismiss it and say, 'I expect I just imagined that!' Whenever you feel them around, send out a loving thought to them. Talk to them and let them know that you are aware of their presence. You can speak aloud if you want to but you can just as easily say the words in your mind because they will be able to read your thoughts.

Don't worry that you can't see or hear them. Spirit communication is a very subtle thing and often works by impressions and sensations rather than words or clear visions. Just try to feel the love they are bringing you and send that love back to them. Later, you may be able to establish contact through a medium. But for now, simply accept that this is your own personal, soul-to-soul communication, your reassurance that they are only a thought away.

2

THE UNBROKEN BOND

'The majority of parents whose children have died have visions of that child within a year of the death. These visions often bring about a lessening of grief for the parent.'

That is the opinion of Dr Melvin Morse, the American paediatrician and expert in near-death studies, writing in his book *Parting Visions*, and I have found it to be the case in my own work. It is very common, as I have said, for mothers especially to feel that their children are still close because of that special mother–child bond which is stronger than death.

Catching Glimpses

The visions may be fleeting. You see your child for a split second, then they vanish. Or perhaps you don't see them clearly at all. You catch sight of them out of the corner of your eye and when you turn your head to look, they have gone. Experiences like this can be startling or even frightening. The usual reaction is to think that you imagined it or that your mind is playing tricks. But if you know that it is real, it is very comforting. What better proof can you have than seeing your child with your own eyes?

Linda Teague, from Devon, had a vision of her son Jonathan, who was killed by a drunk driver. Some time after his death, she was driving with her husband and family past the spot where he had been killed, when something made her look up:

> It was very quick. I didn't realise it was happening until it was all over. He was just there – not standing on the ground. He was wearing his jeans and his favourite T-shirt, the clothes I still have by my bed. There was a beautiful blue sky all around him. It was peaceful yet sad. There was a look in his eyes I can't explain – a look of surrender. He knew there was nothing he could do about what had happened. He walked away into that blue. I didn't say a word all the way home in the car. It wasn't until we got in that I asked my family, 'Did you see Jonathan?' But no one else had seen him. Whenever I see that particular blue colour in the sky, I feel so close to him.

Astrid, who was mentioned in the last chapter, told me how she saw her son Patrick the day after his death, when she was travelling from Stockholm (where she lives) to Oslo, where he had been killed:

> I took the first train to Oslo again Monday morning. I was devastated, shaky and felt like I had been run over by a truck. It was a physical reaction. The pain was almost unbearable. I knew in my mind he was somewhere, yet I felt this incredible pain. I tried hard not to cry on the train and just sat there with my world shattering around me. Then, midway between Stockholm and Oslo, at a station called Karlstad, I saw him waving at me on the platform. I thought it

was my imagination, but it was quite real. There he was beside me for a brief while, indicating all was well.

I saw Patrick several times after that. I caught glimpses of him, though I couldn't be sure if I was imagining it. Sometimes it felt like someone was touching my cheek and chin. One night, when I was sitting by myself looking at his pictures in my album it was as if he was sitting right next to me, telling me to remember the good times and not to worry. At the beginning of April, after he had been gone for two months, I was sitting at the kitchen table trying to get some work done. I was half drowsing. Then I saw him sitting at the table beside me. It was only for a few seconds. He wanted to talk. He was full of love. I woke up as if I had gotten an infusion of energy. It made me so happy. It was as if he wanted to say, 'I haven't gone far away.'

Sceptics may dismiss such visions as delusions but Kate Speed's story cannot be written off so easily. Kate's son David took his own life while deeply depressed. A few days later, her husband Harold saw him:

It was dusk. Harold went into the lounge and there he was, sitting on the end of the sofa. He was so astonished he didn't know what to do. David was shimmering, much lighter than the rest of the room. He saw his clothes. He was wearing dark green trousers and a purple coloured top. There was something white on his feet. Harold was so taken aback by the vision that he didn't even tell me about it until days afterwards. I believed him completely, but I couldn't understand what David had on his feet – he never wore white shoes or trainers. The mystery

was solved when we saw the statement of the police
who had found him. At the time of his death he had
been wearing dark green trousers, a purple T-shirt
and white socks.

Another common phenomenon is smell. You may catch a
whiff of a smell you associate with your child and wonder
where it is coming from. Norma's daughter Giuliana died of
cancer at the age of twenty. The morning after the funeral,
Norma, her husband and her other daughter all smelt incense
in the kitchen. As a Roman Catholic family, they took this as
a sign that Giuliana was all right. On a more down-to-earth
note, one mother said that she often smells hamburgers and
chips in the car – this was her son's favourite treat!

Hearing a Voice

The most common phenomenon of all, and the one about
which parents seek my advice most often, is that of hearing
a voice. Susan told me:

> It was about three months after my son died. I was
> very depressed. I didn't care what I looked like. I had
> just let myself go. Then, one day, I heard my son's
> voice. He said to me, 'Mum, you look a mess!' It was
> so clear that I spun round, though I hadn't heard it
> aloud. It was just what he would say – he liked me to
> look smart. So I made an effort and tidied myself up
> and, from then on, I started to feel better.

These voices vary in type. Sometimes it is an audible voice
that speaks to you or calls your name, but it is much more
likely to be a voice inside your head. Often it is not possible
to make out the words. It could perhaps better be described

as a thought impression. You just know what is being said. Here again, the question arises, 'How can I be sure that it is not my imagination?' It may reassure you to know that even mediums have this difficulty sometimes. Words and thoughts do float up from our subconscious minds and it can be difficult to sort out which are coming from the subconscious and which are from spirit so you must allow for a certain amount of confusion. After all, it is not easy for those in spirit to communicate with us. But there are certain indications you can look for, that will help you to distinguish between real and imaginary voices.

For instance, if the voice or impression drops into your mind at a time when you are relaxed and not even thinking about your child, it is more likely to be real. If it cuts across your train of thought and says something unexpected, or if expressions come to you that are not expressions you would normally use, then they probably don't emanate from your mind. And, of course, if you are told something you don't know and that you later find to be true, this is your proof that your child really is getting through to you. I can only repeat what I have said before. Trust your intuition and your heart.

Dream Meetings

It is common for parents to have very vivid dreams of their child. This is only to be expected and, of course, most people would say that dreams are no more than products of the imagination. Most of them are, and when you have just lost someone you love it is natural to dream of them because they are constantly in your thoughts. But there is a kind of dream – and anyone who has experienced it will know what I mean – that has a special quality about it. It feels real and vivid, as though you were meeting your loved one face to face.

These dreams are more than imagination. When we sleep, our soul or inner being leaves the physical body. This is demonstrated in what are called out-of-the-body experiences, for which there is good scientific evidence. In this state, we can be with those in the spirit world and see and hear them as clearly as when they were on earth because, for that short period of time, we have moved into their dimension.

Usually when we wake up we forget all about these dream meetings or only remember distorted fragments and it is hard to decide whether they were real encounters or just ordinary dreams. Here again, you have to trust your intuition. If the experience was very real, then you were probably with your child. Those in the spirit world often use dreams as a means of communicating with us. In our ordinary waking state they find it very hard to make any impression on our minds but when we sleep we can be together with no barriers between. They must often wish that there was some way they could fix the meeting in our memory!

If you are having frequent dreams of this sort, it is worth keeping a dream diary. As soon as you wake up in the morning, or if you wake up during the night, write down every dream you can remember, whether it was about your child or not. Alternatively, keep a tape-recorder by your bed and speak into it, then write up your experiences later in a notebook. By doing this over a period of time, you will increase your ability to remember your dreams. Then you will be more likely to recall any dream meetings, which will give you and your child a precious contact.

Meaningful Coincidences

Even more subtle than the signs I have mentioned so far are what you could call the 'meaningful coincidences' that tend to occur at this time. For instance, you turn on the radio and hear your child's favourite record being played or you open a book or magazine at random and see a picture that evokes a particularly poignant memory. Are these just chance happenings or are they hints that spiritual forces are at work?

Jack and Lynne Heston chose for the funeral of their son Martin a couple of pieces of music by Jean-Michel Jarre, a composer whom Martin particularly admired. They selected the pieces at random but when Martin's friend Paul heard them he was amazed. These were exactly the same pieces of music he and Martin had selected for a musical project they were working on together – the name of which was 'Life Goes On'. No one but the two boys had known about this.

There may also be signs that you are being cared for and guided. You feel an inexplicable impulse to do something or go somewhere – and it always turns out to be right! One mother felt impressed by her dead daughter to go to a shopping centre she didn't usually visit. Although she was in no mood to go out, she followed the inner voice. On the way, she met a friend with whom she had lost touch some time before. It turned out that this friend had also suffered a recent bereavement and the two ladies were able to give each other valuable support.

How the spirit people do these things it is impossible to say, but they have their ways of guiding us in the right direction, if we can be sensitive to their subtle little promptings. Children have a habit of getting you to do what they want, and it is a habit that persists into the next world!

As with dreams, it is a good idea to keep a diary and make a note of all these things as they happen. Each individual event may seem trivial at the time, and by itself might be no more than chance, but if you write them down, you will be able to look back later and see how they all form a pattern. This will give you a permanent reminder to keep by you for those days when you feel most hopeless and full of despair.

Signs in the House

Some children give quite tangible indications that they are around. They may be heard in the house or their things might be moved. If anything like this should happen to you, don't be frightened or think that they are unhappy ghosts come back to haunt you. It is just their way of letting you know they are there. Children being what they are, if they are ignored, they are likely to persist until they have your full attention!

Lynne Smith's son Richard, who was yet another victim of a road accident, was a weight-training enthusiast. One night some time after his death, his father heard Richard's equipment clinking, as though someone was using it. On another occasion, Lynne's other two sons were in a room belonging to Stephen, the youngest son, when they heard footsteps coming up the stairs. They thought it was their father coming to complain about the noise they were making but when they opened the door there was no one there. They decided it was Richard coming to join them.

Linda, whose vision of her son Jonathan was described earlier, had another experience a few weeks later:

> One morning my husband and I were both woken up
> at three o'clock by the sound of stones being thrown
> up at our window. When Jonathan came home late,
> he used to throw stones at the window to wake us up.
> I said to my husband, 'It's Jonathan. Let him in.' He

went downstairs but there was no one there. I told my mother what had happened. She said that she and my father had been woken at their house, in the same way.

It is not only young children who play these tricks. Kathleen and Bernard Bloomfield's son John died in his thirties of a brain tumour. Kathleen told me:

He was very fond of Mississippi mud pies which I used to make for him. One day I was making these pies to take to a family party. As I was grating the chocolate in a dish, it was as though someone gave the dish a hefty bang from underneath. It leapt about a foot into the air. There was grated chocolate everywhere!

It is interesting how these incidents often involve electrical equipment. There is a connection that we don't fully understand between psychic and electrical energy and those in spirit sometimes seem able to affect electrical appliances. Linda recounted an incident which included yet another of these 'meaningful coincidences':

One day a week after the funeral, when I felt I was going to collapse with grief, I put on one of Jonathan's CDs. It was Dire Straits. The words seemed so appropriate – 'There's always laughter after pain, there's always sunshine after rain'. At that point, the player stopped. I thought that the plug had come out. As I went over to look, it started playing again. This happened three times. I just know this was Jonathan telling me.

Lorraine's son Wayne had been fond of electrical gadgets. Several times after his death, she told me, the video programmed itself to record a programme he always used to watch. One day when she was sitting at her kitchen table she had a shock:

> There was a box of tissues on the table. As I watched, one of the tissues started to move as if it was being tugged. Another day, when my husband Richard was sitting by himself, a paint brush rolled along the window ledge. He said, 'If that's you Wayne, roll it back again.'And as he watched, it rolled slowly back.

Messages in Balloons

My favourite story was recounted to me by a medium from Surrey, Annie Johnson. It concerns two mothers, one in Britain and one in Germany, both of whom had lost sons. It is all about balloons.

Isabel Mühleisen, from Germany, lost her beloved son Frank in 1991. He died of a brain tumour. There are few mediums in Germany and at the end of the year, Isabel phoned a medium in London, Joan Macleod, for help. Among other things, the medium told her, 'Frank wants to have a red balloon in his room.' This made Isabel smile. Frank had been fond of playing with a football in his room and, because it had hit everything in sight, Isabel had suggested jokingly that he use a balloon instead. She did as he requested and bought a red balloon. A day later she phoned Joan and was surprised when Joan told her that she herself had found a red balloon by her back door.

This could have been coincidence, but more was to come. On Isabel's fiftieth birthday she and her husband were on holiday in Switzerland. They had parked the car on a

mountain road and walked off when Isabel remembered
something she had left in the car and went back to get it. As
she did so, she saw a blue balloon coming directly towards
her, which wedged itself between the car and the ground.
There were no children nearby to whom it might have
belonged.

Two years later, Annie was visiting Isabel in Germany.
Annie gave Isabel a sitting in which she mentioned the name
Donald, which she said would be significant. The next day
they went off on a sightseeing tour of Bonn, where they met
an acquaintance of Isabel's, who had also lost a son. As
they were talking, all three of them saw a blue balloon coming towards them. Instead of following the laws of physics
and flying straight, it went round in a bend and flew into
Isabel's arms. To her astonishment, she saw that the word
'McDonalds' was printed on it.

The following year Isabel came to England and she and
Annie went to visit Valerie, who had lost her son Mark.
Isabel was recounting the story of the balloons and Valerie
thought how wonderful it would be if she could have a balloon as a sign from Mark. Isabel expressed a wish to visit
Mark's grave so they set off, Isabel and Annie travelling in
the first car, Valerie and her husband Ian following behind.
Halfway up the high street of the town where Valerie lives, a
blue balloon floated out of the sky and lodged itself under
Annie's car which had stopped at the traffic lights. It was a
Saturday evening and there was no one about. Isabel jumped
out of the car and picked up the balloon which she handed
to Valerie, as a gift from her son. Today, some time later,
Valerie still has it and it has not deflated.

On the way home, Annie gave Isabel a little message
from Mark. 'I have to give you the colour orange – I don't
know why.' The next day they went to visit Annie's friend
Eve. When they were close to Eve's home, driving through
empty streets, Isabel saw something orange floating on the

pavement. It was a balloon. She picked it up and took it back to Germany with her when she returned the following day.

A few months later, she was returning home after another trip abroad. A few minutes after she arrived, some friends who were staying nearby, came to her door by taxi because they had forgotten the address of their hotel. As she went to speak to the taxi driver, she saw in front of the taxi, a red balloon – Frank's way of saying 'welcome home'.

These are just a few of the dozens of stories I have been told by parents, who in many cases never believed in life after death before but were forced to reconsider because they couldn't ignore the things that were happening to them. It is this sort of indication that their child is around that often prompts parents to seek the help of a medium. This is the beginning of a search that takes them into what I suppose most people would regard as strange territory – though it's not so strange when you get used to it. And it is their growing understanding of the life beyond that pulls them out of the dark pit of despair and puts them on the road to recovery. Read their stories and weigh up the evidence for yourself.

3

MY CHILD CAME BACK TO ME

David and Jean Ingman's son Stephen died at the age of twenty-six. It was a terrible blow, as his short illness struck without any prior warning. David would have described himself at that time as a very down-to-earth person, utterly unromantic and even cynical. As the director of a sizeable group of companies, he had to keep his feet firmly on the ground. Before the tragedy, he hadn't believed in life after death, but what happened next completely changed his outlook:

> Two weeks after the funeral, I was out walking with Jean when I heard Stephen's voice in my head saying, 'It's OK. You're over the worst. I can go now.' I was amazed. I turned to Jean and said, 'I've just heard Stephen's voice.' She didn't know what to think. Then I thought, what a harsh thing to say! But when I reflected on it, I decided that Stephen had probably chosen his words carefully. He knew my sceptical turn of mind and that, if he had said something I expected to hear, I would have dismissed it as imagination.

The incident was a turning point for David. That night he slept peacefully, for the first time in weeks. He didn't know where Stephen was or how he had been able to speak to him but he knew that something had changed within himself. There was a mystery here and he was determined to get to the bottom of it.

That was the beginning of his quest. He started ringing round people he knew, asking for help. Always he seemed to be guided to the right person at the right time. Five weeks after Stephen's death he went to his local Spiritualist church in Kent:

> I arrived five minutes before the service was due to begin. While I was sitting waiting a woman came up to me and asked if I was new there. Then she suddenly looked at me very strangely, took me by the arm and led me to another room. She explained that the minute she had heard my voice she had heard the words 'son' in her mind and 'that's my dad'. To my utter amazement, she started transmitting words from Stephen. This time, they were just the sort of things he would have said. She explained that she was the secretary of the church, not a professional medium, but that Stephen had been so insistent that she decided that she must speak to me before the service started.
>
> When she had finished, I went back and attended the remainder of the service. The medium who was taking the service spoke to a number of people present and told them about people from the next world who she said were with them. She didn't speak to me then but later, as she was leaving the church, she said to me, 'There's a young man standing with you with blue eyes and lovely blond hair.' Stephen had been very proud of his hair. The girls at the

discos where he used to go liked to run their fingers through it. As she spoke she was looking below my eye level, at the right height for Stephen, who was shorter than me.

From that moment on, David was convinced that Stephen had survived death and he made up his mind that he was going to establish contact with him. He went to a local medium for a private consultation or sitting. She produced a whole stream of names and information, all of which were relevant but there was one thing that David did not understand:

> She referred to 'Snow White and the Seven Dwarfs'. My critical faculties came into play and I thought about who we knew who had children. Jean's brother has two small children so I asked him. He told me that his daughter was taking part in a play at school – they were putting on *Snow White and the Seven Dwarfs*. This couldn't have been a case of the medium drawing information from my mind. The simple explanation is that Stephen had been to my niece's school and had seen what was going on.

This pattern of evidence was to continue. David went to see other mediums and received more evidence. Ron and June Heron, two well-known mediums who work together, told him, among other things, that Stephen was talking about 'a bungalow and a house'. Four days before he died, Stephen had moved out of David and Jean's house into his own bungalow:

> Ron said, 'He's showing me a window at the side of the bungalow.' I thought there might be something wrong with one of the windows so next day Jean and I went round there to check. What we found proved

Ron right. The owners of the bungalow were in the
process of selling a piece of land at the side to build a
house. They had put up a temporary structure in the
garden, incorporating a window frame, so that the
local planners could see the degree of overlooking of
neighbouring properties. So there was, 'a window at
the side of the bungalow'.

A sitting with the Danish-born medium, Marion Dampier-
Jeans, produced another piece of surprising evidence. Marion
told him that Stephen was giving her the word 'Laguna'.
David didn't understand this and put it to the back of his
mind:

> Two weeks later, I was helping out at a local charity
> event when I felt an irresistible urge to return home. I
> sat down, wondering what I was doing there when a
> Royal Mail van arrived with a registered letter. It
> referred to a planning application for a piece of land
> near our property in Florida. The name of the unit
> developer was Laguna. Who but my son would be
> able to travel 4000 miles, to bring me a piece of
> evidence to prove that he still knows what is going on
> in my life?

Public Meetings

David's story is by no means unusual. Many parents
have sought and received clear proof that their children are
still with them and this has made a tremendous difference to
the way they feel.

'This knowledge has saved my sanity,' one mother told
me. 'I don't know how I would have coped without it.'

I have heard similar comments again and again and it is for this reason that I always urge parents to be open-minded about life after death and to seek the evidence for themselves.

One way of doing this is to attend one of the public meetings, called demonstrations of clairvoyance, that are put on from time to time in halls and theatres by mediums such as Stephen O'Brien who tour the country. These meetings can serve as a useful introduction, especially if, like many people, the idea of going to see a medium privately makes you nervous. It should be borne in mind, however, that not all mediums work to a good standard and that even the best of mediums finds it very demanding to work under these conditions. The presence of a crowd of people, some of whom are only there out of idle curiosity, does not provide a very suitable atmosphere for the spirit world to communicate in. But if you are singled out for a 'message' and if the medium is on form, what you are told may surprise you, as Kathleen and Bernard Bloomfield found when they attended a meeting taken by the famous medium Doris Collins. Kathleen wrote to me:

Our son John died of a brain haemorrhage. Six weeks after his death, we went to one of Doris's meetings in Maidstone, Kent. We were amazed when she came to us. She felt her head in the way John used to do after his operation for a brain abscess three years before his death. She said, 'This person died very suddenly and very quickly. He didn't know that he was going to die and neither did you. He had everything to live for. He had been ill three years before and had been to hospital but he didn't die in hospital. He says you carry a wallet of photos of him in your handbag. He sends his love to his wife and to Peter.' [Peter was his best friend.]

Doris then added, 'Did you buy him a watch? He says that he would like his dad to have it. It would be no good to his wife, though you would find it hard to ask her for it.' In fact, John's wife had bought John a watch. The night John died, she offered it to Bernard but he declined. However, after that message, he asked her for it again and he wore it until he himself died last year.

Some time later, another medium with whom we had a private sitting told us, quite correctly, that John died alone and added that he hit his head on the bedside table. She also told me, from John, that I have some blue tablets that I have difficulty in swallowing, something I had been talking to my son about the day before he died.

We went on to see other mediums, all of whom described John's character and mentioned his age (he was in his early thirties). The messages were typical of him – they showed his gentleness and courtesy and his concern that we shouldn't reproach ourselves in any way because there was nothing we could have done to have prevented it.

Stephen O'Brien's Evidence

Stephen O'Brien, who is the best-known medium in Britain today, told me the following story in which two brothers were reunited by poignant evidence of survival after death.

Stephen was taking a large theatre demonstration of mediumship on one of his nationwide tours when he was contacted by a young lad who gave him the name of Paul, and told him that he had a mum on earth and a brother called Simon, whom he wished to contact. Paul said he'd been killed driving a Yamaha motorbike, which he should not have been riding. He informed Stephen that he was seventeen when he died, on a motorway, during a rainstorm.

Even though these details were quite precise, Stephen said that in these demonstrations delivered in huge, darkened auditoriums, such factual evidence is sometimes met by blank stares from several hundred pairs of eyes. He therefore asked the young communicator to give him more information to place the contact. Immediately, the spirit lad obliged. 'I want to get a message to my brother, Simon, and to my mother Shirley,' he told Stephen. 'She's in the back row of the stalls.'

No sooner had Stephen relayed the mother's name than a young woman's hand waved from that part of the theatre. She explained that she was a close friend of Paul's mother and she was able to verify everything Stephen had said.

'Paul tells me that you visit his mother quite regularly,' Stephen went on. 'You sit in the kitchen and have a cup of tea and a natter.'

'Yes, we do.'

'Well, he often sits with you and listens to all the gossip!' This comment made the audience chuckle, probably at the thought of how many unseen witnesses might be eavesdropping on their own private conversations each day!

'Paul says he's tried very hard to contact his mother and brother, directly – but when he speaks to them, they just can't hear him. And this really bothers him because they're so unhappy when they think of him as dead, and he wants to tell them that he's not dead – he's still alive!'

'I'll tell them for him,' responded the young woman.

Stephen continued:

He sends his love to his mum and brother. 'Tell them I didn't die; I only moved away into another place.

Tell them not to think of me in my last moments – all tangled up in the bike – but to remember me as I was before that – as I am now: healthy, all in one piece, strong and handsome again!

Tell my mum I love her; she's the best in the world. My family were always kind to me, and they gave me a great send-off. I'm nearer to them now than I ever was. And tell Simon to stop feeling guilty about my death. It was Simon's bike that I rode: I took it without him knowing. I shouldn't have taken it. Tell him it was my own fault – and not his.'

From the back of the theatre, the recipient replied, 'Yes, he did steal his brother's bike and then he had the accident.'

Stephen concluded with: 'Paul says, "I don't want Simon to keep having nightmares over what I did. He feels guilty – he shouldn't feel that. Tell him I said so. Tell him that I love him."'

Attending a Spiritualist Church

The best way of finding out about life after death and seeking your own evidence is to attend a Spiritualist church. As I have mentioned, there are hundreds of churches around, particularly in the London area. Some of them have their own premises, while others meet in hired rooms. Your local church should be listed in the phone book but, if not, the Spiritualists National Union or the Greater World Christian Spiritualist Association (see Useful Addresses) will be able to tell you where your nearest church is.

There is nothing secret or hidden about Spiritualism. Anyone can go into a church and attend one of the services or evenings of mediumship. Churches also offer spiritual healing, which brings relief on all levels, mental and emotional as well as physical, so it can be of great help at times of bereavement or stress.

Perhaps, like most people, you would never think of setting foot inside a church, except for hatching, matching and dispatching. If this is the case, please try to overcome your reluctance. The services are quite simple and informal. You will not be subjected to long boring sermons and no one will pounce on you with an ardent desire to save your soul.

Nor do you need to be afraid that you will find any weird rituals going on inside. Services are conducted in normal light and you won't see any ghosts. The people are quite normal too and you can be sure of a warm welcome. Many people come into Spiritualism when they have lost someone close to them so you are bound to find people with whom you have a common bond. You will be able to discuss any psychic experiences you have had and no one will think you strange. For many parents, there is a great sense of relief in being able to talk about these things with people who understand. Spiritualists regard contact with the dead (who, of course, are not really dead at all) as something quite natural, and after a few visits you will begin to realise that it is not as bizarre a notion as you may once have thought.

Every Spiritualist service includes a demonstration of what is called clairvoyance – in other words, mediumship. The medium will pick out various members of the congregation, describe those from the spirit world who are with them and pass on a short message. It has to be said that these demonstrations can be very disappointing. Unfortunately, the standard of mediumship in churches is not as high as one would wish. This is not because the mediums are dishonest. Most of them are sincere and well intentioned. But their ability is limited and all they are able to give is vague generalisations that could apply to anyone, or snippets of

information which, while they may be correct, are of little
relevance or value.

If, on your first visit to the church, you find the medium uninspiring, don't be discouraged. Every service is taken
by a different visiting medium so try again or try another
church. You may have to sit through a few indifferent demonstrations of clairvoyance before you see one that really
impresses you but your patience will eventually be rewarded.

'Messages' in Churches

Some of the best mediums I have seen are those who work
quietly in Spiritualist churches and never become known to
the general public. Anna O'Donoghue, who lost her son
Francis in a road accident, visited a Spiritualist church in
Bristol. It was her first visit to the church and no one there
knew her. She was surprised when the medium singled her out:

> The medium suddenly announced that she had a
> young man with her who was sad because he had
> died in a motorbike accident recently. She said that
> the young man was telling her that he had been going
> too fast and that the accident had been all his fault.
> She said he wanted to say how sorry he was about his
> carelessness. He then offered a rose. To me it was
> obviously Francis: he had died in a motorbike
> accident, he was young, I always put roses on his
> grave. It was subsequently proved that he crashed
> because he was going too fast but I did not know this
> when I visited the church.
>
> Before Francis came through, the medium contacted
> an old lady who she described as small and bird-like,
> dressed in old-fashioned clothes with a high collar

buttoned round the neck. She told me that this lady
was my great-grandmother and that she had died
because she had something wrong with her throat. In
fact at this point the medium clutched her own throat
in a dramatic choking fashion.

I asked my mother about this lady as I had no idea
who it could be. My mother told me it was indeed my
great-grandmother, who was exactly as described and
had died of cancer of the throat. She was called
Eliphalette Wrench. I only knew her by name and did
not know what she looked like or how she had died
and for a long time could see no connection between
Francis and her. However, I told a relative, Sally
(Eliphalette was her grandmother), the story. Sally
was very interested and sent me a photograph of her
grandmother who looked exactly as described by the
medium. Even so, for a long time I could not see any
connection and I put the photograph in a glass-
fronted cupboard where I keep various treasures.

One day, a few months later, still puzzling over the
message, I took the photograph out of the cupboard
and turned it over. I noticed, for the first time, that
somebody had written on the back, many years ago,
the words 'Eliphalette Wrench, mother of Francis'.
(Francis was Sally's father.) One mother of Francis
communicating with another mother of another
Francis?

Another touching story was sent to me by Denise Gregory
of Bath. Mrs Gregory's mother visited a local Spiritualist
church where the medium spoke to her:

The medium said to her that there was a little girl
showing herself with my mother who had a circle of
flowers on her head. My daughter, who was six when

she passed, was looking forward to being a
bridesmaid. As her head-dress had already been
finished we put it on her head in the coffin.

Yvonne Pellvet received great help from Jo Benjamin, one of
the most famous mediums of his day, who died a few years
ago. Her stepson John was killed in a flying accident at
Biggin Hill:

For three years after it happened, I was on
tranquillisers. I walked around like a zombie. I had
no one to talk to. The Vicar was very kind and I went
to church but it wasn't giving me what I needed. I
needed to know that John was still alive. One day I
decided that I had to get help. I went to Jo Benjamin
for spiritual healing and stayed for the demonstration
of clairvoyance afterwards. I thought it was a load of
rubbish but the friend I went with pleaded with me to
go again.

The second time I went, John came through. Jo said
he could hear a whirring noise, like an engine cutting
out. Then he said, 'I've got a young man here. He is
fair with curly hair and blue eyes, about five foot five
in height, a very handsome young man. He did well
in school, he got four A-levels and thirteen O-levels.
He was an accountant. He keeps calling for his
mother.'

My friend nudged me. 'That's John!'
I was too amazed to speak but eventually I put up
my hand and said, 'I'm his stepmother.'
'He went through the windscreen of an aero-
plane,' Jo went on. I could not believe what I was
hearing. This man did not know me from Adam yet
he was giving me all this information. I could not
stop crying.

'He is fine now,' Jo told me 'He's working on the other side to help people who have died in accidents or other tragic ways. Don't see his passing as a loss.'

Those words set me off on a new pathway in life. I immediately stopped all the pills I was taking. From there, I went on to join a Spiritualist church. I became a healer, and now I work as a medium.

I could cite many more examples of this kind, showing how much evidence for life after death does come through, evidence so precise that it cannot be explained away as wishful thinking or guesswork on the part of the medium.

Help from Unexpected Sources

When you set out on this spiritual search, help sometimes comes in surprising ways. Like David, you may find that you are guided to meet people who can help you. When Ron and Christine's son Aaron was killed abroad in a diving accident, they, like most bereaved parents, had no idea where to turn for help. Christine told me:

I neither believed nor disbelieved at the time – I had never had any need to think about it before. I went to my local priests for comfort but they were no use at all. All they told me was that I had to have faith. They made me so angry that I almost threw them out of the house! I was having some work done in my home at the time and I found myself talking to the builder about what had happened. It turned out that he was a medium. He helped me a lot and recommended me to go to a Spiritualist church. My other son and I started going there regularly. Ron, my ex-husband, sometimes came with us. We're still good friends and we were able to support each other.

One of the mediums from the church came round to see me at home. Aaron did not come through on that particular occasion, though we did get evidence of other relatives. But at the church we went from strength to strength. We got numerous messages from Aaron from various different mediums. What was so striking was the way his personality was described to us again and again and the way he frequently referred to things that were going on in our lives.

Ron took up the story at this point:

On one of my visits to the church, the medium said to me, 'There is a young man standing with you. He is your son. He was abroad when he passed and you had to bring his body back. He is smiling and saying that you should not have bothered – you should have left him there.' Then the medium described the accident. 'He was going deeper and deeper. He didn't realise how deep it was. Then it all went wrong and he was drowned.' That was exactly how it happened. The medium had never seen me before.

He went on to talk about our divorce and said that his mother has a new family now. He said that my son was saying that he was sorry about the accident and asking me to forgive him – he had no one but himself to blame. Then the medium said, 'He still walks with you in the woods in the morning.' There are woods near to where I live and we did walk there together – I still go there every morning.

4

PRIVATE SITTINGS

It is hard to convey in writing the impact that this spirit contact with their children has on the lives of parents. Only those who have lost a child know the depth of pain it causes and only they know the comfort of realising that their child is alive and happy in another dimension. This is especially true for parents who had no previous belief in life after death. David Ingman said:

> When you first lose them, you think that they are
> gone forever, but when you hear from them, it's
> wonderful! The grief is so much lessened. Then you
> have to reprogramme your thinking to get used to the
> idea that all you have lost is the physical presence and
> companionship – that they're happy where they are
> and wouldn't want to come back. Once you accept
> that, it enables you to get on with your day-to-day
> life. This life is a learning experience, so let's make
> the most of it! We'll see them again one day, then
> we'll have eternity to be together.

If you want to investigate Spiritualism, it is not enough to rely on the short messages given at public meetings. You will need to go for a private sitting with a medium. Sittings usually take place in the medium's own home, so the conditions are much more favourable. The medium will be able to concentrate their full attention on you and your spirit communicators, without the distraction of an audience.

Your church will be able to recommend a medium, or, if you live in London, you could go to one of the Spiritualist organisations – the Spiritualist Association of Great Britain, the College of Psychic Studies or the Greater World Christian Spiritualist Association – all of which offer private consultations. If you cannot find a church where you live, the Spiritualists National Union will be able to give you the address of the nearest church or centre. If you live abroad, you should get in touch with the appropriate organisation in your country. You will find a number of addresses at the back of this book.

Bear in mind what has been said about the standard of mediumship and be prepared for the fact that you may need to see more than one medium before you find the proof you are looking for. But choose the people you see carefully and resist the temptation to spend all your time rushing from one medium to another. This will only result in frustration and disappointment. Don't let your search become an obsession. Your child does not want you to become so preoccupied with trying to contact them that you neglect your own life and the people here who need you.

Some parents are put off by the fear that they will be taken in by fake mediums who are taking advantage of their vulnerability. Unfortunately, such people do exist. There is no law to stop anyone setting themselves up as a medium or psychic and charging whatever fee they like – or think they can get away with. These charlatans bring into disrepute the vast majority of honest mediums and they do incalculable harm because they leave parents more distressed, confused and sceptical than ever. Do not go to any medium who advertises her services like an end-of-the-pier fortune teller, or who 'guarantees' results. Mediumship is a vocation that true practitioners treat with seriousness. And, because it is a delicate gift, and cannot be turned on and off like a tap, no honest medium will 'guarantee' good results on every occasion.

Bernie's Story

Bernie Metcalfe, who wrote to me from the Wirral, had some bad experiences before the conviction she was looking for came to her in a very strange way. She and her husband began their search, following the death of their son Liam, by visiting the Spiritualist Association of Great Britain in Belgrave Square, London:

> We were very apprehensive, particularly when the medium we saw told us that he might not be able to contact the one we wanted. He proceeded to tell us many accurate details, such as that my husband was wearing Liam's clothes and that we had travelled to London in his car (both true). He couldn't get his name or how he died. The one thing that clinched it for my husband was when we received a message from his friend George, who had been killed in an accident at work, a few weeks before Liam's death. This contact was a complete surprise as George was the last person that we were thinking of. My husband left quite happy that this was enough proof, but all it did was to leave me wanting more.

Bernie started doing the rounds of all the mediums who advertised in local papers, but with little success. One

medium in particular made her angry. The sitting was quite
expensive but was far from satisfactory. A few weeks later,
the medium phoned Bernie and invited her to attend a meeting she was taking at a local venue. At the beginning of the
demonstration, the medium asked for 'Liam's mum' and
handed her a silk rose, 'from your son, with love', to the
applause of the audience. Bernie, who had told the medium
her son's name at her sitting, understandably felt exploited
at this blatant cheating and vowed never to have anything to
do with mediums again. But her son found another way to
get through to her:

> Some time later, my mum and dad were shopping in
> another town and felt compelled to go into a pub for
> lunch, very unusual for them. During their meal, they
> noticed a lady watching them, and as they were
> leaving, she approached them, explaining that she
> didn't usually accost people in pubs but that she was
> a medium and that Liam had pointed them out to
> her as his Nan and Pop (Liam's name for his
> grandad). He wanted them to tell his mum Bernie
> that he was all right and he was often with her when
> she was crying. They were completely gobsmacked!
> She took their phone number in case she needed to
> contact them again. It was almost six months later
> that she phoned to tell them that she was guest
> speaker at a local Spiritualist Church if we wanted to
> go, which we did.
>   I had never met her and was surprised to see this
> ordinary lady telling us all that she was like most of
> us, had a job, did her shopping in Asda, liked a night
> in watching the telly. She then asked for a Metcalfe,
> and when I acknowledged her, proceeded to
> bombard me with totally accurate information about
> Liam, his girlfriend, his sister, his uncle who was

more like a brother (there was only two years between them), the fact that we had moved since he had died, his cat had died, all meaningless to anyone but ourselves. She mentioned that Liam had died on a very special day (he died on the feast day of Our Lady of Lourdes, Liam visited Lourdes many times and had a great faith). She finished by assuring me that his face was OK. (At the end the leukaemia had gone to his brain and twisted his face, rather as though he had had a stroke.) I sat completely open-mouthed, tears of happiness pouring down my face.

I have since had a private sitting with this lady, at no cost, and she was again staggeringly accurate. I derived an enormous amount of comfort from her, during a particularly distressing time. I have not been again, but know that she is available should I need her. She made a tape of the sitting which I often play on bad days, just to reassure myself that Liam is all right and is still very much involved with our lives. It's not quite the same as having a conversation with him or seeing him, but it is the next best thing. I firmly believe that Liam chose this lady to work through, for whatever reason.

Bernie's story illustrates the need for caution in investigating mediumship. But, as I have said, mediums like the one she encountered who behaved so badly are rare and are vastly outnumbered by the sincere mediums who do their work to the best of their ability. So don't be discouraged by any setbacks or failures. Remember that your child will be reaching out to you and will probably, like Liam, be determined to get through one way or another. All they need is for you to give them the opportunity.

How Soon Should You Have a Sitting?

If you have only recently lost your child, you may be wondering how long you should wait before having a sitting. People are sometimes advised to wait for a few weeks, as it is often thought that it takes this amount of time for anyone who has passed into the spirit world to be able to communicate with those on earth. I don't altogether agree with this advice. It is true in some cases but it depends upon the individual and how strong their links are with those they have left behind.

When a child goes on a journey away from home, for a holiday or for some other reason, the first thing they want to do when they arrive is to ring home and let their parents know they have arrived safely. It is the same with the journey into the spirit world. Their first thought is to get in touch with their parents. Being children, they won't want to wait.

My advice, therefore, is to have a sitting as soon as you feel ready to do so. However, don't expect too much from this first attempt. Regard it as an introduction. It is like the first phone call home – a chance to say 'hello' and 'don't worry about me'. But don't be disappointed if you don't get much more than that. Should the sitting be a complete failure, as sometimes happens, or should your child not come through at all, do not assume that there is anything wrong or that they don't want to speak to you. It may just be that they need a little more time. Book another sitting a few weeks later but do not give up your quest. You will find that, as time goes on, they come through more clearly, until you are left in no doubt that they are with you.

Going to See a Medium

People are often apprehensive about going for a sitting. They don't know what to expect or what is going to happen. They may think they are going to find a dark room, with the medium in a trance. In fact, nothing spooky happens. Sittings take place in normal light and few mediums go into a trance – I personally have never gone into a trance in my life!

Mediums cannot make spirits appear. Some people who come to me have the idea that their deceased loved ones are going to materialise in front of their eyes. I don't know if they are relieved or disappointed when this doesn't happen. All a medium does is to talk to the sitter, describing the spirit people he or she can sense and passing on whatever they want to convey.

If you ever feel your child close to you, catch a glimpse of them or hear their voice inside your head, you are in fact doing what a medium does. The only difference is that mediums have a greater degree of psychic ability, which enables them to communicate more clearly. But, however good the medium, it is never as clear as one would wish. Mediums don't see spirit people suddenly materialising any more than you do, nor do they hear their voices like listening to the voice of someone on earth. It is much more subtle and delicate than that.

It is, in effect, a mind-to-mind contact, a sort of telepathy. The person from spirit who wants to communicate has to impress their thoughts and emotions upon the medium's mind. The medium receives this information in various ways. Sometimes it comes in words, sometimes in the form of mental pictures. Often, it is just a sensation or an emotion. All mediums have a slightly different way of working but, if I explain how I work, perhaps that will give you the idea.

Before I begin the sitting, I have to make my mind quiet and still. I must set aside all thoughts of the everyday world, whatever is going on in my own life, and try to make myself receptive to the world of spirit. I say a prayer, asking God and my spirit helpers to make me a clear channel of communication for the sitter's loved ones. I then try to raise my thoughts to the spiritual dimension. This is rather like turning the knob on a radio so as to pick up another station.

When the sitter arrives, I talk to them for a few minutes, putting them at their ease if they are nervous and telling them what is going to happen. Then I endeavour to sense who is with them from the spirit world. Sometimes I may see who is there – not clearly but in a hazy outline. Sometimes I may get a picture of them in my mind. More often, I pick up an impression of the character of the person who is trying to come through. This impression may be very vague at first but, as I go on, hopefully it becomes clearer. I may hear them speaking, as a voice inside my head. All these impressions I pass on to the sitter. Taken together, they should allow the sitter to identify who it is.

I also pick up the spirit communicator's emotions. Some people are very emotional, especially when they first make contact. Children are often very excited at being reunited with their parents and I often find my own eyes filling with tears as I link in with them mentally. But they are tears of joy, not of sorrow.

Difficulties in Communicating

As you will have gathered by now, mediumship is a delicate art. However much they may want to communicate, the spirit people are limited by the medium's ability to receive what they are trying to convey. This can cause a number of difficulties which may make sitters question whether they really are making contact.

Parents may wonder, for instance, why their child doesn't come back to them through a particular medium, when that medium is perhaps able to accurately describe other members of the family who are in the spirit world. It may well be that the child is there as large as life, if you could only see them – but that they are unable to make the medium aware of them.

On other occasions, you may find that the medium does make a link with your child, and tells you certain things that are quite correct but fails to mention obvious and important things that would be the first things you would expect them to talk about. In fact, your child may be trying to say what you expect to hear but they just can't get their thoughts through. On the other hand, insignificant and trivial details may come through quite clearly.

Another point that worries parents is that the medium, while perhaps describing the child's character exactly, may be unable to pick up their name. This seems surprising. Surely, if someone is seeking to prove that they are there, the most obvious way to do so is to give their name. But this may not be easy. As I have said, mediumship is mind-to-mind communication. It is simpler for those in spirit to transmit a mental picture, a thought or an emotion. To convey something abstract, like a name, is more difficult, although, of course, it can be done if the medium is sufficiently well attuned to the spirit world.

No medium is 100 per cent accurate in what they say; nor can any medium, if they are honest, guarantee to get good results every time. If the contact doesn't flow naturally, there is no point in trying to force it. All a medium can do on these occasions is to admit to the sitter that they are having difficulties and suggest that they try someone else. It is no one's fault. There are many subtle factors involved in communication, some of which we don't fully understand, and each sitting has to be regarded as an experiment.

The Role of the Sitter

You, as a sitter, have an important part to play in the success or otherwise of the consultation. It is no good being impatient. Trying to communicate can be a very frustrating business, not only for you but also for your child or whoever is seeking to contact you. It is just as frustrating for the poor medium who is doing their best but is only able to give you as much as they are receiving themselves. If you adopt a highly sceptical approach, this will set up a barrier, as it creates a cold, analytical atmosphere which makes it hard for the medium to work. This is not to say that you should be gullible either. Assess everything you are given with an open mind. Recognise that, because of the nature of mediumship, it is not possible to dot all the i's and cross all the t's although, if the sitting is working well, all or nearly all of the information given should make sense to you and should be accurate and helpful.

If you are highly emotional – and, understandably, parents are extremely distressed and emotional following the death of a child – this can also cause problems. Depression, tension and any intense emotion creates a fog around your mind that is very hard for the spirit people to penetrate. Try to keep your emotions calm and peaceful and don't pin all your hopes on one particular medium or sitting.

Take notes or tape-record the session, as you are unlikely to remember everything that transpires and sometimes things that seem trivial at the time can prove to be significant later on. If you are given any information that you are unsure about, concerning your child or other people from spirit, try to check it out and see if it is true. Keep a record of all your sittings so that you can read them back at a later date; then you will see how the evidence has built up.

Most parents find that what convinces them is not just the factual information, vital though this is, but the way in which one medium after another will describe their child's personality, perhaps using their pet expressions, or referring to things that are happening in the family, which show their continuing concern with those on earth. Ron told me:

> My son Aaron was very anxious that I should forgive him. Several times, soon after he passed, we received messages to say that he was sorry for the distress he had caused us and that he had no one but himself to blame for the accident. He also spoke of his concern for his mother, who was going through a particularly bad time and for his brother, who he said had to sort his life out, which was quite true. All the messages made sense in relation to what was going on in our lives at the time.

Sometimes they will tell you of something personal known only to you and them or give you some piece of information that you know nothing about. Valerie received a very telling piece of evidence concerning a watch:

> The medium said that my son Mark was talking about a gold watch and saying that it was his father's watch which he had been wearing when he was killed. This was quite true. When the police brought Mark's possessions to our home after the accident, the watch was among them. I didn't know this at the time, since my husband Ian had taken the watch and hidden it, knowing it would upset me. Mark said to Ian,

through the medium, 'The watch is in the third
drawer down of your dressing table, on the left-hand
side.' Ian doesn't actually have a dressing table but he
does have a desk that looks similar and he had
hidden the watch exactly where the medium said.

Pat French's Story

It is hard enough for a parent to lose one child, but some of
the parents I have met have lost two children and yet have
found the strength to cope. Pat French lost both her sons in
separate road accidents. Her eldest boy, Nicholas, was killed
in 1989, the very night before Pat and her husband were due
to leave for Spain, where they were to open a restaurant.
They had bought a house, their furniture had gone on ahead
and the restaurant was waiting for their arrival. They didn't
know whether to go or to stay in England but, on the advice
of friends, they decided to go and start the new life they had
planned.

Pat wanted to see a medium but couldn't find one in
Spain. However, her step-daughter had a sitting at which
Nicholas came through with a message for her. Pat told me:

The message gave me tremendous encouragement,
especially as it came when I wasn't even present.
Nick said, ' Tell Mum I'm with her all the time. I'm
OK – all in one piece. It's great here – I can do just
what I like. I can still ride a motorbike.' Nick had
loved his bike. He said, 'I would have been crippled
if I'd stayed – No way!' That was typical of him – he
would have hated to live like that.

When she came back to England for Nicholas's funeral,

Pat had a sitting with another medium and got a lot more comfort. Then, in 1995, tragedy struck again. Her second son, Damian, had a fatal accident on his motorbike. Pat returned to England for the inquest and while she was in the country she went to see a medium who described Nicholas to her:

> She said, ' There's a young boy here who was killed in an accident. He wants to say that he passed extremely quickly – there was no pain. He's saying they turned the life support machine off and that this was the right thing to do. I feel that every bit of him has been used. Was something donated? because he's saying, 'People live on because of me.' He's giving me the date of the 28th. He's got his jeans and white T-shirt on – he looks so smart.'
>
> All this was quite correct. Nick was in intensive care for a few days before the life support machine was switched off. I agreed for his organs to be donated because I knew this was what he would have wanted. The 28th was the date of his funeral.
>
> Another medium brought Damian to me. ' Was this an accident?' the medium asked me, because he never felt anything. He was happily going along and suddenly he was there with his brother. You wrote something to him, because he's got it. He's saying, 'You daft nelly!' I had written a poem to Damian and put it in his coffin. That was just what he would have said about it.
>
> I had various other sittings, some of which were more successful than others. Even though none of the mediums knew anything about me, they described my sons' characters exactly – they were such different personalities – and gave me some remarkable messages. One of them named Damian's two favourite football teams, Manchester United and

West Ham – Damian was football-mad. Another said that Damian was into body building. I didn't know anything about this, but when his things were sent back to me from the Air Force base where he was training, there were body building weights among his things. I may not have my boys in body but I know that they are with me in spirit – it's so comforting.

Answering the Critics

Critics of mediumship claim that it is wrong to encourage parents to seek contact with their children because of the painful emotions it can stir up. It is true that it can be distressing for parents when they are unsuccessful in their quest, either because the mediums they see are not very good or because, owing to the difficulties I have described, it is hard to establish contact with the child. This lack of success can leave parents more confused and doubting than ever. That is why I warn people to be very patient in their search and to choose the mediums they see with care. I warn them also of the problems of communication, so that they have some idea of what to expect and don't have unreasonably high expectations.

It is also true that there can be a tantalising feeling of being 'so near and yet so far' when the medium makes some contact with the child but doesn't give the parents the evidence they are looking for, or if they themselves sense the child's presence and are unable to see them. But nearly all parents, if they persevere, do find evidence. And, in my experience, those parents who know that life goes on after death cope with their grief better than those who believe that death is the end, because they know that they have not lost their children for good.

Critics also suggest that mediums make it harder for parents to let their children go and to resume their own lives. Here again, I disagree. I do occasionally come across parents who are constantly having sittings with mediums as a means of clinging to their children because they cannot bear the thought of being parted from them. And, like most mediums, I try to encourage such parents, as gently as possible, not to become centred on this contact but instead to turn their attention back to their own lives and the people here who need them. But it is only a small minority of parents who do this. In general, once parents are satisfied in their own minds that their children are still living and that they are well and happy, their need for 'messages' diminishes. They may still have sittings from time to time to keep in touch, in the same way that, if their child had gone to live in a foreign country, they would still want to hear from them. But the urgent need for contact is replaced by a calm knowledge that their children are getting on with their own lives in the spirit world and that they should now do the same.

Developing Spiritual Awareness

Once they have this knowledge, parents often develop a spiritual awareness of their own which helps them to feel closer to their children. The ability to be aware of those in the spirit world is not some rare gift, nor is it anything mysterious. It lies dormant in many people. In the majority of cases, it remains dormant for the whole of their lives. But when something shattering happens like a bereavement, a person's whole way of thinking is turned upside down. Suddenly material things don't matter any more and they start to look for something beyond. As they do this, it is as if a curtain lifts. They become more open, more receptive, and the ability that has been hidden within begins to grow and reveal itself. Then those they love, who have been patiently awaiting their opportunity, are able to come close to and make themselves known.

In *Contacting the Spirit World*, I explained how to develop this awareness for yourself and suggested some exercises to try, but here is a simple meditation exercise to start you off. You will need just one piece of equipment – a candle. Some soft background music may also help.

Choose a time when you are by youself and not likely to be disturbed. Early morning or last thing at night is best. Light the candle, then sit quietly for a few minutes and take some deep breaths while you listen to the music. Relax completely. Start with your toes. Tense the muscles, then relax them. Then tense and relax your feet and ankles. Move up your body, tensing and relaxing each part in turn. Then relax the mind. Try to let go of all the stress and anxiety of the day. Though it may be difficult, try also to let go – just for a few minutes – of the grief and sadness. Let it all float away from you until you are completely calm and at peace.

Now gaze at the candle. Don't stare at it, just rest your eyes gently on the flame for about half a minute. Close your eyes and you will see the after-image of the flame. Hold this in your mind's eye until it disappears, then open your eyes and gaze at the candle again. Do this three times. Every time your mind wanders, bring it back to the candle.

The object of this exercise is to still your thoughts completely. It is impossible to make your mind go blank so, instead, you give it an object to focus upon. By keeping your concentration fixed upon this object, you will eventually find a point of stillness within. You may need to practise this exercise every day for a few weeks before it has an effect, but if you keep at it, the stillness will eventually come.

At this point you will begin to become spiritually aware.

This awareness is a delicate thing, hard to describe in words. You will not go off into a trance or see wonderful visions. You will simply feel an inner peace, a certainty that there is something beyond the material things of life.

Rest in this peace and, as you do so, you may become aware of the presence of your child or other spirit loved ones around you. Do not strain for this or try to force it. And do not expect to see them or hear their voices. Just send out love to them and feel their nearness. By doing this, you will be building a bridge of communication with your child. The more you practise this, the stronger that bridge will become.

In time, you may be able to hear them speaking to you, but I cannot promise this. Not everyone is able to develop the ability to hear. But you should, if you meditate regularly, reach a point at which you will know that your loved ones are there and feel united with them in your thoughts. This inner knowing, this communion of the heart, as it has been called, is a very personal thing. It is something deep within you that you cannot prove to anyone else. But, because it is so close to your own heart, it will in the end give you a greater conviction than you could ever obtain in any other way.

Developing the Gift of Mediumship

As you continue your spiritual search (having sittings and growing more aware of the spirit world), you may wonder whether you could become a medium. It is quite possible that you might. The inner knowing that I have been describing is in fact the beginnings of mediumship. Now you may want to find out whether you can develop this further.

In order to do this, you need to join a psychic development circle. This is a group, led by an experienced medium, in which beginners are trained. To find such a group, make enquiries at a Spiritualist church or centre. If you join – and the person leading the group will probably want to interview you to assess whether or not you are suitable – be prepared for a lot of hard work. It can take years to become a good, reliable medium. You can use certain techniques in order to attune your mind to the spiritual dimension, and I have described these in *Contacting the Spirit World*. But it all comes down to patience, quietness of mind and meditation – slowly building a bridge of communication with the spirit world.

If you do discover that you have this gift, you will soon find that you are drawn to use it for other people. Some of the best mediums I know have begun their work in this way, following a bereavement in their own lives. There are so many people who are in need of this special kind of help, and if you can assist others to find comfort, then your efforts will be richly blessed – and no doubt your child will be working beside you, reaching out to those in need.

When parents come to see me following the death of a child, they are always anxious for information about the child's passing. 'Was he afraid?' they want to know. 'Is he all right now or is he lost and alone?' On this point I can give them reassurance. Death is no more than a gentle transition from one dimension to another. We know this from those who have had near-death experiences and also from those who have passed beyond death and come back to tell us about it.

5

STAIRCASE TO HEAVEN

Katie was nine when she fell into a swimming pool. She was rushed into intensive care, where a scan showed she had a massive swelling of the brain. The doctor who tried to resuscitate her, the American paediatrician, Dr Melvin Morse, had little hope of saving her life but, against all the odds, she recovered. When she was feeling better he called her into his office for a follow-up examination. He asked her what she remembered about her near drowning and was amazed when she replied, 'Do you mean when I visited the Heavenly Father?'

With Dr Morse's gentle encouragement, Katie revealed more details of what had happened while she had been unconscious and close to death. She described how she saw the doctors trying to resuscitate her. Then a tunnel opened up and through it came a beautiful woman whom she called Elizabeth. Elizabeth took Katie through the tunnel. At the other end she met her grandfather and other people she knew who had died. At one point, she was taken back to her home where she saw her brothers and sisters playing with their toys. After her recovery, she was able to describe to them exactly what they had been doing. Finally, she said she was taken to meet God and Jesus. God asked her if she wanted to go home again. She said no, she wanted to stay with him. Then Jesus asked her if she wanted to see her mother again. 'Yes,' she replied. And with that she woke up back in her body again.

Katie had had a near-death experience. During the time when she was so ill that her body showed no signs of life her soul had left her physical being and travelled into the land beyond death. Her case is by no means unique. Near-death experiences (NDEs) have been reported for hundreds of years. In the last twenty or thirty years they have been intensively studied by doctors and psychiatrists. Thousands of accounts have been collected from all over the world, from people who have come very close to death or who have been physically dead and have been resuscitated. These accounts are remarkably similar, even though the people concerned have been of widely differing beliefs, ages and nationalities. Thanks to what they have told us, we are now able to build up a plausible picture of what it is like to die.

NDEs usually conform to a typical pattern. At the moment of death, the soul slips out of the body like a hand out of a glove. The person then finds themselves hovering near the ceiling, looking down at their body below. Initially they are frightened but this fear is soon replaced by a sensation of peace and euphoria in which all their anxiety melts away. If they were in pain before, they notice that the pain has vanished and they are wrapped in warmth and contentment.

They are, however, quite lucid and can see everything that is going on around the body. Some people, on returning to physical consciousness, have astonished doctors and relatives by describing in detail the efforts being made to bring them round. Others, like Katie, have left the place where the body was lying and witnessed events taking place in their own homes or in distant locations.

The separation from the body is followed by the next

stage of the NDE. This is usually described as travelling at great speed down a long dark tunnel. The tunnel represents the transition from this world to the next. Again, there is no fear associated with this, rather a sense of being loved and protected.

Some people perceive the tunnel as a corridor. For others, it's like being in outer space. Sometimes it is seen as a staircase. A young boy who died during heart surgery confided to his mother excitedly when he was revived, 'I have a wonderful secret to tell you. I have been climbing a staircase to heaven!'

At the end of the tunnel there is a light. This is like no light on earth. It is dazzling but does not hurt the eyes. In this light a being is waiting. He is majestic yet kindly. Some call him God or Jesus. Those of non-Christian faiths might see him as Buddha or some other celestial being. There are other people there as well, deceased loved ones who have come to greet the dying person on their arrival.

A few people are given glimpses of the spirit world as they stand on this threshold. They say that, in many ways, it looks like this world, except that it is far more beautiful. In fact it is so beautiful that they want to stay there but they are told, either by the being of light or by one of their loved ones, that they must return because it is not yet time for them to go over. They then wake up in the body again.

Not all NDEs follow this pattern. Some people who have a close brush with death do not experience anything that they can remember. Others only get as far as the tunnel before returning to consciousness. A small number of people have what are called negative NDEs, which are unpleasant and frightening, but these cases are a tiny minority. Almost without exception, people who have had an NDE claim that it was beautiful and peaceful and that it has taken away forever their fear of death.

Typical NDE Accounts

Here are a couple of typical NDE accounts both given by
children. This is the story of Mary Lowther, quoted in *The
Truth in the Light*. Mary was eleven when she almost died of
acute peritonitis.

> I remember still, with total clarity, the feeling of utter
> overwhelming peace and tranquillity. I was looking
> down on myself in the bed, my mother sitting beside
> it, and my father standing by the window. I knew he
> was crying. I seemed to 'float' along a corridor
> towards, then into, all-enveloping brightness and
> light, with indefinable shades of pastel-like colours.
> There were what I can only describe as billions of
> beautiful shimmering forms, no outlines, and they
> were all 'cloaked' in what looked like a garment of
> translucent light.
>
> The most wonderful thing was the music, which
> I can only describe as almost a tangible joy
> emanating from, yet part of and encompassing these
> forms, of which one appeared to be the source and
> somehow embraced all else. Another impression was
> the vastness, no horizon, no 'cut-off points';
> infinity, I suppose, is the best description.
>
> I longed to be able to tell my parents not to
> grieve, that if they could only know how joyously
> happy I was they would rejoice instead. For that is
> the dominant feeling, the memory and knowledge of
> ultimate, total peace. So death can come at any time
> and holds no fear for me as a result of what I consider
> to be a privileged experience.

The American NDE researcher, Dr Raymond Moody,

interviewed a boy called Jason who had an NDE after being hit by a car. Jason's account is given in *The Light Beyond*:

> I don't remember getting hit but suddenly I was looking down at myself. I saw my body under the bike and my leg was broken and bleeding. I remember looking and seeing my eyes closed. I was above. I was floating about five feet above my body and there were people all around. A man in the crowd tried to help me. An ambulance came. I wondered why the people were worried because I was fine. I watched them put my body in the ambulance and I was trying to tell them it was fine but none of them could hear me. I could tell what they were saying. 'Help him,' someone was saying. ' I think he's dead, but let's go to work,' said someone else.
>
> The ambulance drove off and I tried to follow it. I was above the ambulance following it. I thought I was dead. I looked around and then I was in a tunnel with a bright light at the end. The tunnel seemed to go up and up. I came out on the other side of the tunnel.
>
> There were a lot of people in the light but I didn't know any of them. I told them about the accident and they said I had to go back. They said it wasn't my time to die yet so I had to go back to my father and mother and sister.
>
> I was in the light for a long time. It seemed like a long time. I felt everyone loved me there. Everyone was happy. I felt that the light was God. The tunnel whirled up toward the light like a whirlpool. I didn't know why I was in the tunnel or where I was going. I wanted to get to that light. When I was in the light I didn't want to go back. I almost forgot about my body.

When I was going up in the tunnel, two people were helping me. I saw them as they got out into the light. They were with me the whole way. Then they told me I had to go back. I went back through the tunnel where I ended up back in the hospital where two doctors were working on me. They said, 'Jason Jason.' I saw my body on this table and it looked blue. I knew I was going to go back because the people in the light told me.

NDEs in Children

NDEs in children do not differ substantially from those of adults. There is, however, one feature of the NDE commonly reported by adults that is usually lacking with children – the 'life review'. Many adults state that, at some point after entering the light, they saw their lives flash before them like a video being replayed. As they watched they saw all they had done wrong; the times when they had taken the wrong path. They were guided through the review by the Being of Light but he did not condemn them. They judged themselves and felt very remorseful as they became aware of their faults and mistakes and the pain they had caused to others.

Older children may have an experience of this kind, but young children seldom, if ever, mention a life review. They are probably too young to have much to regret!

Children who are shown the spirit world during their NDEs speak of a place of love and harmony. One child who died at the age of seven told Dr Morse:

I was in a beautiful place with flowers and rainbows, where everything was white like it had its own light. I was talking to several people while I was there, including Jesus, who wanted me to stay with him. I wanted to stay there, but we decided I had to come back and see my parents again. I'm not afraid to go back to that place.

Cherie Sutherland, an Australian researcher, quotes in her book *Children of the Light* this account from a woman who had an NDE when she was twelve. At first all she could see was darkness, then a comforting hand descended and carried her up into the light until they reached a beautiful garden:

We stopped in the middle of the garden. I looked around, and oh my goodness me, I have never in my life seen such a beautiful place. There was peace, and I couldn't describe the serenity. Just beyond description. So I looked around – it was a beautiful place – everything seemed so calm and peaceful and lovely. Suddenly I saw among the beautiful flowers, butterflies, so many of them, big huge ones all flying around. And I thought, O look at that! There was one so beautiful, with beautiful golden wings. I said, 'Oh, I love that one.' And I wanted to catch it.

She was just about to get hold of it when she heard her name being called and felt someone shaking her. On opening her eyes, she saw the doctor looking at her, an expression of relief on his face.

'She has come back to us,' he said. But the girl didn't know what he meant, or where she had come back from.

Many children speak of their meeting with the Being of Light. Some of them see this being as an angel, though he does not have wings. For other children, he is Jesus, but he does not necessarily look like the traditional Jesus. One child informed his father that he was not at all like the Jesus he had seen in the Christmas nativity play! But whoever he is, he radiates love and the children feel secure and happy with him.

They also meet deceased relatives and friends there. Katie met her grandfather. Sometimes they meet relatives they do not recognise, who have died some years before. One girl met a child who said her name was Olivia. Later, when she told her mother about her NDE, she was surprised to learn that Olivia was the name of an older sister who had died before she was born. Even family pets may be there, since animals also survive death and accompany their owners into the Afterlife.

There is no disease and no pain in this world. For children who are ill, it comes as a wonderful release. They can run, jump and play.

'You'll see,' one young child enthused to Dr Morse. 'Heaven is fun!'

Perhaps it is not surprising that these children do not want to come back. Some of them say they were given no choice in the matter and were sent back because there was work for them to do on earth. Others were allowed to choose themselves and decided that they had to come back for the sake of their parents. One little boy said that he returned to his body because his parents had already lost his younger brother and he did not think they could cope with losing him as well.

NDEs can occur at any age. Dr Morse cites the case of a three-year-old boy who remembered an NDE he had when just nine months old, in which he had crawled up the tunnel into the light. Children who have NDEs are profoundly affected by them. They have been touched by the light of the spirit world and the light remains with them. Compared with other children of the same age, they are more mature and view life in a more spiritual way. Material things do not matter much – they have glimpsed a higher reality. Death holds no fear for them. Jason told Dr Moody, when asked how he felt about what had happened to him, 'To me, I died. I saw the place where you go when you die. I am not afraid of dying. What I learned there is that the most important thing is loving whilst you are alive!'

Into the Spirit World

For a parent whose son or daughter has passed into that greater world, reading about the near-death experiences of children can be a tremendous source of comfort. It reassures them that their own child did not suffer in making their transition to the other side of life. Children who come back through mediums also say that leaving the physical body was easy and painless. They too speak of being drawn up into a beautiful light that enfolds them in warmth and love.

Russell Byrne, who died of cancer at the age of nine, told his mother, through a medium, how he woke after his death to find a beautiful lady standing in front of him who picked him up in her arms and told him she was taking him on a journey. She lifted him up and it seemed to him that they were walking on air. Presently, he saw a light in the distance which he realised was the entrance to a tunnel and they walked through the tunnel out into a beautiful light:

> My eyes were dazzled at first, but as they grew
> adjusted to this great light I could see things. I could
> see other children. I could see other people that were
> beloved of mine on the earth plane, waving, smiling,
> greeting. I found myself, Mum, in this wonderful,

wonderful garden . . . like a cross between a garden and a park land. That's the nearest I can describe it upon earth. It was so light, it was like a glorious summer's day, but it wasn't too hot and it wasn't too cold. It was just perfect and there was such love in this place.

Children are Never Alone

No child is alone at the moment of death. This is important for parents to know. Even if they themselves were not able to be at the bedside – perhaps because they were not able to get there in time – someone from the spirit world is there with every child, to help them gently over. Often it is a grandparent who does this, or some relative whom the child would know and love. If there is no one in the family with whom they would be familiar, they are met by a spirit helper (like Katie's Elizabeth), who takes care of them.

A child who dies suddenly, as a result, for instance, of a road accident, may at first be shocked and confused, not able to understand what has happened to them. Strange to say, they may not realise at first that they have died, since the spirit body, in which we are clothed after death, looks and feels like the physical body. Help is always at hand, however. The spirit world always knows when someone is going to pass over, so someone will be there to meet them. There may be some sadness at parting from those they have loved on earth but the peace of the spiritual world eases the trauma and they are taken to a place of healing.

In some cases of violent death, the transition to the next place is so gentle that there is no awareness even of leaving the body. In *On the Death of my Son*, Mike Swain, a teenager killed in a car crash, tells his father how he and his young passenger, Heather, felt no impact as the cars collided. They were surrounded by a golden light and lifted up out of the car:

> Heather and I are still holding hands. We now descend beside the Mini. We see two crumpled bodies lying in it. We feel vaguely sorry that this should have happened to them. And we both fully understand that we are now, as far as mortals are concerned, dead. We are also both aware that a lot of people have begun to gather round us. They are dressed in glorious colours. We recognise familiar faces; the faces of friends who passed beyond the earth before us. We are still hand in hand now, guided by the one who first lifted us into the air, the two of us sweep towards the skies.

This spirit world into which the children have gone is not far from the earth. Thanks to the gift of communication that joins the two worlds, we know quite a lot about what it looks like and the lives children live there. But in order to understand the nature of this world, we have to discard a lot of what most of us have been taught about death.

6

CHILDREN IN THE SPIRIT WORLD

When I was very young, we had a family ritual. Once a fortnight, my parents and I would go to the cemetery where my mother's parents were buried. We would stop at the entrance by the rusty tap and fill one of the watering cans provided. Then we made our way up the winding, overgrown path to the grave, me clutching a bunch of flowers. My grandparents' memorial was a simple cross, inscribed with their names and underneath, the words, 'rest in peace'.

Solemnly, my mother would remove the old flowers and I was allowed to arrange the fresh ones in the vase, while my father trimmed the long grass around the grave. Then we stood in silence for a few minutes, while I remembered my grandmother and thought about my grandfather, who had died before I was born.

'Are Nan and Grandad down there?' I once asked my mother.

'Yes, dear,' she said.

I thought about this. 'It can't be very comfortable.'

'Er . . . well . . .' My mother changed tack slightly. 'They're not actually there, just their bodies.'

'Where are they, then?'

'They're in heaven.

'Where's that?'

'Heaven? Well, it's . . .' She appealed to my father for help.

'It's up in the sky,' he muttered vaguely.

'What do they do in heaven?'

'They play harps,' my mother told me, 'and sing hymns.'

This was what the scripture teacher in school had told me. It sounded rather boring.

'Will I go to heaven when I die?' I asked.

'We're all going to heaven, dear.'

'What – even the bad people?'

'Well, perhaps not the very bad people.'

'Where do they go?'

'They go to hell.'

Hell had been mentioned in our scripture lessons too and glossed over rather quickly.

'What's hell like?' I asked.

'It's very hot,' my father replied.

'Like Australia?'

'No, dear, not quite like Australia.'

Even at that tender age, I sensed that there was something lacking in this view of the Afterlife but none of the adults around me could come up with any more helpful information. Asking about death produced a similar reaction to asking where babies came from – red faces and shuffling of feet.

Spirit View of the Afterlife

Most of us, as children, were given the same sort of traditional teaching about heaven and hell. It's not a very convincing picture, so it's hardly surprising that people discard these ideas as they grow up, along with their belief in Father Christmas. What we are told by spirit communicators about the next world paints a very different picture. It appears to be rather like this world, only more beautiful.

It is inhabited by people who are still very human and have bodies that look like earthly bodies. There are no pearly gates and no judgment throne and if there are angels, they don't have wings.

We are told by the spirits that their world is not a place that can be located in our physical space. When people leave the body at death they do sometimes speak, as Mike Swain does, of floating upwards into the sky but they are not actually being taken to a land above the clouds; they are passing into a different dimension.

There are in fact many different dimensions or planes. They can be thought of as a ladder, starting at the earth and reaching upwards, although, of course, they are not physically situated one above the other. When we die, we step onto the first rung of the ladder known as the astral plane. This is the plane that is sometimes visited in near-death experiences. Although it is often assumed that it is heaven, it is only the gateway to the spiritual world.

We stay on the astral plane for some time. There is no fixed rule about how long we remain there. It may be only a few years of earth time, or it may be hundreds of years. It depends how fast we wish to progress. But when we are ready, we begin to climb up the ladder to the higher dimensions beyond the astral. On theses planes, the earth-like conditions give place to a more rarified environment, and the resemblance to earthly life ceases. When we reach that stage, although we retain our individuality, our consciousness is greatly expanded. From this level it is still possible to contact those on earth but this contact does not take place so frequently. When people do come back from this level, they come as teachers or spiritual guardians. Mediums call these spirit communicators 'guides'.

Heaven is the last plane of all, the very top of the ladder, and it takes aeons of time to reach it. It is so far removed from anything we can understand that we cannot begin to imagine what it is like or how life is lived there, though I doubt whether harp-playing features very much! Even the spirits cannot tell us much about heaven because they are so far from reaching that plane themselves. All we know is that it is our final destination, a state of bliss and being at one with God.

What About Hell?

So what about hell? This is, apparently, a place reserved for people who were evil, who deliberately inflicted pain and suffering on others. This region is, however, bleak and desolate, rather than being like the traditional visions of hell. But God does not sit on a throne judging souls as they arrive and consigning sinners to perpetual torment. We gravitate automatically to the plane with which our vibrations are in harmony.

A person who was sadistic or cruel would be drawn to the hell-like regions where he would be in company with like-minded individuals. He would stay in these miserable conditions until he felt remorse for his actions. Then he would be given the opportunity to atone for his crimes, after which he could move on to somewhere better. There is no such thing as eternal punishment. A saintly person would rise straight away to the higher dimensions nearer heaven. But most of us, being neither great saints nor great sinners, find our way to the astral plane that has been described, where we are reunited with those we loved on earth.

The Astral Plane

The most surprising thing about the astral plane is that it appears so material. There is general agreement, both in near-death accounts and communications from the dead themselves, that it has scenery similar to our world, with all the things of nature that give us pleasure: the trees, the flowers, the birds and the warmth of the sun. It is possible to pursue many of the same interests and pastimes we have on earth, such as music, arts and sports.

But, despite this apparent similarity, life there is very different. There is no day and night and there are no changing seasons. Modern devices, such as cars, computers and telephones, are not needed. Spirit people travel by the power of thought and communicate with each other telepathically. Having said that, mechanical things do exist. Pat French's son Nick, for instance, says that he still rides his motorbike. Objects like motorbikes have no real place in the astral world, but the matter of which that world is composed has a curious property. Objects can be created by the power of thought. When people first arrive they may feel the need to have familiar things around them, so these things can be provided. But when they become acclimatised to the spiritual environment they no longer have any desire for them, so they cease to exist.

In the same way, it is possible to eat and drink, although the astral body does not need food. Mike Swain explains:

> When you first arrive here the routines of eating and
> drinking and sleeping are too firmly established to be
> eliminated at one fell swoop. So if you think you
> need to sleep, well, you lie down on a couch in one of
> the houses, and you sleep for as long as you want. If

you think you need to eat, then eat your fill. There
are no excretory organs in our bodies. For example,
when I drink a glass of water, it just diffuses itself
throughout my system, and that's that! In other
words, it's converted into energy. If I see a beautiful
apple tree, with bright red apples on it, I can reach up
and pick one off, and swallow it – all it does is to give
me a tingling sense of satisfaction!

People who live in the astral world – and I call them 'people'
rather than 'souls' or 'entities' – are much like people here,
except that, because of the spiritual nature of that world,
they are generally wiser, more tolerant and more loving than
they were on earth. As the plane is only a step away, it is
relatively easy for them to make contact with the living.
They can if they wish, and if there is a channel of communication open to them, stay closely in touch with their
families, keeping watch over them and being involved in
their lives.

Children in the Astral World

For children, their entry into the astral world is the start of
an exciting adventure. There is so much for them to explore
and discover. Ros Catternack's son told her, through the
famous medium Leslie Flint:

The most exciting thing that could ever happen to
anyone is to die. To die is to live. You couldn't begin
to depict the beauty of the world which I now inhabit
and I am only on the fringe. That's what makes it so
exciting. One never stops learning. There is always
something else to experience.

The astral body, which is the body we wear when we leave the physical form behind, looks like the material body. However, like everything in the spirit world, it is composed of a lighter substance. Children find it great fun that they can run and jump further than on earth.

This body does not suffer any pain or weakness. A child who has been injured in an accident would wake up with no injuries. If he had lost a limb, he would be whole again. A child who had been blind or deaf would be able to see or hear again. Brain-damaged children or those suffering from any form of mental handicap recover their mental faculties. The brain is part of the physical body, and when this is left behind, the mind functions perfectly again.

If a child has suffered from a long, debilitating illness, they might need a short period of rest on first arriving. Parents are puzzled if a medium tells them that their son or daughter is in a spirit hospital and think this means that they are still ill. In fact, these 'hospitals' are places of rest and healing. Sometimes, if the illness has been a particularly difficult one, the mind is worn out as well as the body and, although the astral body is free of any weakness, some healing is needed to cure the mind of the exhaustion caused by the long struggle.

However, being resilient, children don't usually need to rest for long. Some don't need to rest at all, and are up and about as soon as they arrive. When they communicate with their parents, the first thing they say is how radiant they feel. One of Mary Clifford's daughters, Sheila, spent several months before her death blind and in a wheelchair. She came back a few days after her death, to tell her mother excitedly, 'I can run, I can walk, I can see!'

Getting in Touch with Parents

Peter Cowlin, an eighteen-year-old road accident victim, told his parents via a medium:

> When I first awoke to the certainty that I was
> established on another plane of being, one of my first
> thoughts was, 'How can I get in touch with Mum
> and Dad?' You know how it is, when you arrive at
> any destination your first thought is to ring home
> and let them know you have arrived and are OK.

This is the immediate reaction of most children when they get to the spirit world. They see their parents grieving for them and want to let them know that they are safe. For a few days after leaving the body, they tend to spend a lot of time in their earthly homes. Their thoughts take them wherever they want to go, so they can travel easily between there and their new home in the spirit world. If they are not able to come alone, they are accompanied by whoever is looking after them. They can see and hear everything that is going on and are aware of people's thoughts, so if you speak to them in your mind, they will be able to hear.

The first days after death are a transition period, a time when the child is coming to terms with what has happened. They need to feel their parents' loving thoughts and, as I have said elsewhere, it helps them greatly if they know that their families understand that they are still living.

The amount of time they spend close to their families in this way depends on the individual. A child who has not been loved would have little incentive to try to maintain contact at all, but would remain in the spirit world, where he would receive the love that had been lacking on earth. If there is a deep bond with the parents, the child will stay very close until they are over the worst of the shock and grief, helping all he can by sending them comfort.

It is because of the child's strong desire to communicate that even the most un-psychic of parents often feel them around at this time and may catch a glimpse of them or hear their voice speaking in their minds. If there is someone available with whom they can communicate, they will be very happy to do this. In fact, they often prompt their parents to go to a medium, though they find that it is not very easy getting through, especially not at first – the art of communication is as hard from that side of life as it is from this.

Astrid's son Patrick tells of his attempts:

I was so eager to communicate to you just days after my arrival in the spirit world. Yet I didn't know how best to and had to be patient and wait for you to ready yourself. I was helped by your spiritual protector. We made all sorts of plans on how to reach you. I made arrangements for you to meet the mediums you have met. I was a bit excited at first, to see if I could get through. On that first occasion when you met Arthur [the medium], I managed to get through with some pictures and words we had rehearsed beforehand and I was very, very glad to be able to do so. From my side, the first time is like talking under water. You don't quite know if the medium has got it or not. I saw you quite clearly – you were so happy and relieved. We all rejoiced afterwards. It was a breakthrough. After that I got used to it. I was at several meetings with mediums.

All of us, at this stage, want to communicate with loved ones, some more than others, but we are dependent upon the requests and wishes of the parents.

Children's Activities in the Spirit World

Children in the spirit world live with their families: grand-parents or, if the grandparents are still on earth, other relatives with whom they have a bond of love. Those who have no close ties with their own families are taken to live with other people with whom they feel at home. No child is ever lost or lonely.

But what do they do there all day long? This seems to depend, as it would on earth, upon the child's age and inclination. Young children find other young companions to play with. They have toys and games, as well as pets and animals. They are free to enjoy their surroundings, running through the countryside and swimming in the rivers, with none of the dangers that may threaten children on earth. If they are old enough they go to school, where they are taught many of the subjects they would have studied on earth as well as learning about the spirit world and the higher planes of existence. They can, if they wish, visit places on earth. Russell mentions that he has been to see Disneyland, though he adds, 'It was not so magical as anything I'd found in my new world!'

Older children have more mature activities, though exactly what these are is hard to define, as they seem to find it difficult to describe these activities in words that we on earth would understand. Peter Cowlin told his parents:

> Of my daily life here, it may surprise you to know
> that, I too, have my hours mapped out in the form of
> a timetable of intent. We, not being in time, do not
> have a clock mentality, but we do have a system
> whereby intentions are measured out as blocks of

energy, programmed in a way not dissimilar to your time. Thus we have tasks, projects and deadlines to meet in our own energy time system.

Miscarriages and Abortions

Some infants die without ever having touched the earth. Sadly, miscarriages are very common. For a mother, to lose a baby in this way is a special kind of sorrow – a grieving for the child she never knew. Sarah told me about her miscarriage:

I was six months pregnant. It was my first child. I knew something was wrong because the baby hadn't moved inside me all day. I went to the hospital and they did a scan but they couldn't find a heartbeat. I already knew that my baby was dead. The doctors decided to induce the birth rather than putting me through a Caesarean. I was heavily drugged. It was even more traumatic for my husband. They left him sitting outside the ward. He looked at all the little plastic beds with blue and pink blankets for the babies that were being born in the labour wards. All there was outside my room was a stark hospital trolley where our child was going to be put.

It was a boy. They told us that he was perfect, but that the placenta was malformed and he must have died from lack of oxygen. We weren't allowed to see him or hold him. I wished afterwards that I had insisted on seeing him, even if only for a moment. It would have helped. We wondered what they were going to do with the body. In our ignorance, we didn't think to ask.

When I went home, I felt empty because I didn't have another person relying on me any more. He was

a real little person, with his own character. I gave him
a name and talked about him. Eventually, I got over
it and had other children. But I still think about him.

When women are pregnant they often do sense, as
Sarah did, that the child they are carrying is a real person
waiting to be born. The soul exists in the spirit world before
coming to earth. If the birth does not take place because of
some physical defect, the soul is taken by spirit helpers back
to the world it came from. In certain cases these souls,
because they have been deprived of the opportunity to experience life on earth, are born again at a later date. They
may even return to the same mother. In other cases, they
grow up in the spirit world and, like other children, remain
in contact with their mothers.

I am often aware, when giving sittings, of these spirit
children. Because they are unsullied by the earth they
develop into very beautiful beings and bring so much love
and happiness with them.

The souls of aborted children are also taken back into
the spirit world, either to grow up there or to come back to
earth later on, as the case may be. The decision to terminate
a pregnancy is one no woman undertakes lightly. The femi-
nine wisdom that resides in every woman tells her that she is
rejecting the soul within. But if she wanted the child, and
her decision was taken for good reasons, medical or otherwise, the child's soul will know this, and there will still be a
bond to link them together.

Growing Up in the Spirit World

It is sometimes thought that children in the spirit world, like
Peter Pan, never grow up, but in fact they do grow into

adults. Young children are permitted to enjoy their child-hood, but there comes a point at which they have to put away their games and take up some kind of spiritual work.

Mary Clifford, whose daughters Sheila and Gillian both died before the age of twenty, was able to follow their progress through messages she received over ten years:

> Sheila was always motherly. She liked looking after
> younger children and she was given the job of
> helping to take care of the little ones. Gillian was
> more of a tomboy. For a few years after her passing
> she was doing much the same sort of thing she
> enjoyed here. She felt she had been deprived of her
> childhood and she was allowed to play as much as
> she wanted. But after a few years, I was told that her
> grandfather, my father, was saying, 'She's got to settle
> down now and become more serious.' Now she works
> as a teacher, helping her sister.

When children contact their parents through mediums, per-haps several years after their death, they appear to have reached the same age they would have reached had they stayed on earth. Sometimes they do present themselves look-ing as their parents remember them, but this is just done so that they will be recognised. It sometimes happens, when I am giving a sitting, that I get two images at once. I have an impression of a younger child, as if they were saying to me, 'This is how I used to be.' Then I 'see' them as they really are, in their grown-up form.

Because their minds are more flexible than those of adults, children tend to mature quickly in the spirit world. They soon begin to discover greater realities and become very wise and spiritually evolved. If their parents are receptive on a spiritual level, the children can teach them much of a spiritual nature.

In a beautiful book called *Benjaya's Gifts*, Carmella B'Hahn tells the story of her son Benjaya who drowned in a river by which he had been playing. Always a deeply spiritual boy, he soon reached a level of higher consciousness in which, as he told his mother, he no longer felt himself to be a child, although he could still come back to his mother in his original form if he wanted. In the book, he says:

> I am Ben-el-eth, far bigger than just Ben, and I can call upon so much you wouldn't believe. That's how I can be so much help to you, because I can expand my boyself to give almost whatever you want. Actually, it's a bit confusing because it's not like I am a boyself who can get bigger and wiser – that's how it was when I first came here – now I am the whole wiser self and can still come to you as my boyself because that's what you draw from me, like a magnet attracts certain metals . . . Whenever you think of me I know about it and often I come instantly to be with you. It's so easy you wouldn't believe and it's taken me a while to understand how part of me can be clowning around Higher Green and another part is teaching or learning somewhere else.

Parents do not need to fear that their children will become lost to them. Though they grow up in a spiritual sense, they do not lose their individuality, nor do they cease to care about loved ones on earth. While their parents need them, they will never pass beyond their reach.

7

BY THEIR OWN
HAND

The death of a child by suicide brings its own particular kind of problems. The parents' pain is compounded by confusion, guilt and perhaps the fear that the child may be lost or unhappy in the spirit world because of the manner of their death.

The suicide rate among children and young people has risen dramatically over the last few decades. Increasing social pressures, the widespread use of drugs, bullying at school and violence and abuse in the home are cited as some of the causes. Depression and mental illness, which are also on the increase among the young, are major factors. Suicide cuts across all barriers of race and class. The victims may come from disrupted families, in which they have been neglected and subjected to cruelty, but they can just as easily come from stable homes with loving parents.

Such a death leaves the parents with endless questions to which, apparently, they will never be able to find answers. 'Why did he do it?' they want to know. 'What was in his mind – was he frightened, lonely, confused? Why couldn't he talk to me and tell me what was worrying him?' They are unable to comprehend what could have been so bad, so overwhelming, that death seemed the only way out.

If the victim left a note, this gives some insight into their reasons and their state of mind. But the contents of such notes often come as a complete shock to the parents, who had no idea that the child was in such a desperate state. Sometimes there is no note, no clue. It is impossible to be sure whether the death was a determined attempt to end their life, an accident, or a last-ditch appeal for help that went tragically wrong.

When a child dies in this way, the parents are left with a burden of failure and guilt which they may carry for the rest of their lives. They are often convinced that they have let their child down. They torment themselves, thinking that they should have realised what was going on and done something to prevent it. This guilt is made worse if they can see, looking back, that there were warning signs that they might have picked up, had they been more observant, but it is easy to be wise in hindsight. A teenager's depression and withdrawal, for instance, may be deemed to be no more than the moodiness of adolescence. Even remarks like 'No one would miss me if I wasn't here' may have been construed as empty threats. There is a common belief – which, unfortunately, is a fallacy – that people who talk about committing suicide never actually do it.

Another common reaction, though one less readily acknowledged, is anger. 'How could he do this to me?' parents demand. And then they feel even more guilty because they are angry. In fact, suicides are usually so depressed at the time of their death that they are unable to take anyone else's feelings into account.

Attitudes to Suicide

All bereaved parents find that they are shunned by other people, even their friends, who do not know what to say to them and are embarrassed by their grief. This is worse for parents of suicide victims. Until recently, suicide was regarded as a crime – the only crime, it has been ironically remarked, for which you cannot be punished if you are found guilty. The Church viewed it as a mortal sin. Suicides were considered damned and their bodies were not allowed to be buried in consecrated ground.

Fortunately, this harsh attitude is no longer so prevalent, since it is now recognised that anyone desperate enough to take such an action is deserving of sympathy rather than condemnation. But there is still a stigma attached to suicide. Parents and families can find themselves treated as if they were responsible or drove the child to it, and this adds to their own feelings of guilt.

Marilyn's Story

There is no such thing as a typical suicide victim but children who take their own lives are often loving, sensitive people, highly attuned to the feelings of others. There is a vulnerability about them that makes them react severely to knocks and slights that other, more robust children take in their stride. This sensitivity makes them prone to depression. It is as if they find this world too harsh to bear. Many of them are perfectionists who feel inadequate when they fail to live up to the expectations of their parents or their own self-imposed standards.

Marilyn's son Philip, who was twenty when he took his own life by a drug overdose, was one of these sensitive young people. Although he was a reserved boy, Marilyn says that he was sociable and popular with his peers, with a good sense of humour and much loved by his family. She told me what happened:

When he was seventeen or eighteen, he was having difficulty deciding what he wanted to do with his life. He had done voluntary work in the community. The obvious next step was to go to university. He wanted to do some sort of caring work. He was a very caring person.

He was suffering severely at this time from clinical depression which had been coming on for some time. He was intelligent and could have done anything he wanted with his life but he could see no prospects for himself. He was travelling in France with a friend when he had a nervous breakdown. We went to France and brought him back. He was obviously very sick.

The doctors at the hospital where he was treated put him on anti-depressants. I knew he was suicidal and I was worried that they were handing out so much medication to him but they assured me that he could be trusted not to take an overdose. After a few months, he seemed to be getting better and we were hopeful that the worst was passed, so, when he did take the overdose, it was a terrible shock. Later, I was told that, when a person who has been deeply depressed starts to feel better, that is a dangerous time because they have the energy then to do it. I only wish they had warned me of this before Philip died.

Suicide Victims in the Spirit World

Parents who come to me following the suicide of a child are often anxious to know whether the child is in an unhappy spiritual state. They may have heard that suicide victims become lost souls wandering the earth and are distressed to think that their child could be in this condition. They may also have heard the theory that we are allocated a certain number of years in this world and that, if a person takes their own life, they remain tied to the earth until their allotted span of years has expired.

It should be said that suicide is always wrong, because the gift of life is not ours to take. Victims may go through a period of unhappiness after death but much depends upon why they did it and upon their emotional and spiritual state. I have communicated with many children who entered the spirit world by their own hand and, though some of them may have needed some help to adjust, they were none of them lost souls. Nor were they earthbound – that is to say, unable to release themselves from the physical dimension.

Nearly always, however, they say that they bitterly regretted ending their lives as they did. They are able, from the spirit world, to see the extent of the suffering they have caused and this saddens them. They are also able to view their lives in their true perspective and often realise that they could have worked things out, had they waited a little longer or tried harder. This regret and self-reproach is something they have to learn to come to terms with. But there is no judgment or punishment for them there, only love, understanding and compassion.

They are helped to review their lives, to understand where they went wrong; and in this review their motives are carefully considered. Someone who, like Philip, was suffering from an illness such as clinical depression would not feel the same remorse as a person who acted on a thoughtless impulse.

'I never would have got better,' Philip told his mother, through me. 'I didn't want to put you through any more suffering.'

As I linked mentally with him, I felt that he was at peace and at home in the spirit world. In fact, he told his mother that he now works to help other young suicide victims on their arrival after death.

Communicating with Suicide Victims

Suicide victims feel a great need to get in touch with those they have left behind, to say that they are sorry and, in many cases, to explain why they acted as they did. Their need to communicate is so strong that their families are aware of their presence and pick up their distress, hence their anxiety as to the child's state.

'I feel him with me constantly,' one mother said of her son. 'I know he's trying to tell me something but I can't hear what it is.'

It is in situations like this that a medium can help so much, by providing a much-needed channel for them to speak to each other. I am always glad to be able to do this, but I have found that it is not always easy to make a link with suicide victims. People who have taken their own lives seem to experience more difficulty than others in getting through to a medium and this sets up a slight barrier. However, once this is overcome, they are just as capable of communicating as anyone else.

This particular lady's son wanted her to forgive him, which she willingly did, and simply to tell her that he was all right. This was all he needed. As soon as the contact had been established, I felt his relief. Thereafter, his mother continued to feel him with her very often. But, instead of the heaviness she had detected when he first came back, he brought with him an atmosphere of joy and happiness.

Shirley's Story

It is often assumed that suicide is a phenomenon associated only with teenagers and adults. Sadly, this is not the case. The Samaritans, Childline and other support groups are receiving more and more calls from young children. Studies have shown that children as young as three can suffer from severe depression and feel that their lives are not worth living.

One of the most moving stories related to me while I was compiling this book was from Shirley, whose son Oliver took his own life when he was only eleven years old. Shirley began her story:

> Oliver was a very intense child, highly sensitive and intuitive. He was very fond of his brother William, who was four years younger than him. He was a deep thinker. We used to have long talks about God and religion. I used to say to him, 'Oliver, not even my friends talk to me like this.' And he was also very psychic. I was always aware of my father's presence. One day he said to me, 'Mum, your dad isn't really dead. He's in this house.' But he treated it as something quite normal. He felt deeply for other people and took on their problems. Some of the things he saw on television really upset him and he used to cry about them.
>
> His problems started when he went to high school. It came as a real shock after the more easygoing environment of his junior school. He did well academically. In fact, he worked very hard. He always wanted to get top grades. But some of the teachers frightened him and he was bullied by the other boys because he was sensitive and pretty and because the girls liked him, which made them jealous.

On his first day, he said to me when he came home, 'I can't go on. I can't cope.' I was very worried about him. I told him he had to learn to put on a defensive armour, to appear tougher than he actually was. He looked at me with those piercing blue eyes and said, 'That's terrible!' He couldn't bear any pretence or dishonesty. I complained to the school about the bullying but nothing was done and Oliver never did learn to retaliate when he was attacked.

He told me, 'I'm going to end it all.' Other people didn't believe him. They said, 'He doesn't mean it, he's too young.' But I knew he was serious and I was frightened for him. I promised to take him out of the school as soon as I could. After half term things seemed a bit better and I thought he was adapting. I didn't realise that he was putting on a veneer.

One day, he came home very upset because of something that had happened in school that day. The class had been talking about what was going on in Bosnia. He got very upset. He said, 'How can people be so cruel to each other?' After dinner, he said he was going up his room. I put William to bed and read him a story. When Oliver didn't come down, I thought he must be playing with his computer. I went up to his room and opened the door. He was hanging there by his school tie. William rushed in behind me. I couldn't stop him.

I thought, 'O God, Oliver, you've done it!' I cut him down and tried to resuscitate him. Then I called an ambulance but I knew it was too late. William kept saying, 'I'm so frightened!'

There are no words to describe the shock to a mother of discovering her child's body in such a horrific way. 'You never get over a shock like that,' Shirley told me. 'You learn to accommodate it.' Her only comfort was that she felt Oliver near her, and felt that he was at peace. 'He's where he wanted to be.'

I also felt this when Oliver came through to me in a sitting. The image I had was not of an unhappy child but of a mature and very spiritual being who had been unable to tolerate a world in which there was so much cruelty.

'His passing wasn't in the least traumatic for him,' I told her. 'It was like going from one classroom to another. He was depressed not so much for himself as for the state of the world. He's coming back to you as a teacher, to lead you and your husband to a higher state of consciousness.'

If Your Child Has Committed Suicide

If your child has gone into the spirit world by their own hand, remember that there is a great deal you can do to help them. Most importantly, send them your love. Prayers and loving thoughts sent out from the earth are always received by those in the spirit world. It is also important that you forgive them, however much pain they have caused you and regardless of whether or not you can understand their motives. They may well be regretting what they did and your forgiveness will make it easier for them to forgive themselves.

Speak to them, aloud or in your mind. Remember that you don't need a medium to help you to do this. They will pick up your thoughts, even though they may not be able to make you hear them in return. Sit quietly for a few minutes every day, or whenever you sense that they are with you, and try the meditation exercise given earlier. Picture them in your mind's eye, happy and surrounded by love and light. When you feel ready, find a good medium with whom to have a sitting. Children who pass to the spirit world in this way have a greater need than any others to communicate with their parents and, if possible, to explain why they acted as they did. Making contact helps them to put the sadness behind them and move forward in that world.

Above all, know that they are not beyond your reach and that, despite the tragic manner of their death, they can still find happiness and fulfilment in the world beyond.

8

INNOCENT SOULS

It is heart-breaking for a parent to have to watch their child suffering sickness or mental or physical handicap. Many of these parents sacrifice their own lives in order to give their children all the love, help and support they can but they often feel frustrated and inadequate. They would gladly take the suffering upon themselves, if it was possible.

When Mary's grandson Benjamin was born, he seemed to be a strong, healthy baby. Mary, her daughter Marie-José and her daughter's husband were all delighted with him. The only thing that bothered them was that he was a little too good. He was quiet and docile and rarely cried.

Their concern deepened when the nurses in the hospital observed that Benjamin wasn't taking any notice of the world around him. Various tests were carried out but the results were never made clear to the family. About a year later, a doctor at the children's hospital in Bristol did further tests. His conclusions confirmed their worst fears. He told them that Benjamin was never going to be normal.

Mary continued the story:

Benjamin was a puzzle to the medical authorities. He showed symptoms of autism but he was never

diagnosed as fully autistic. My daughter separated
from her husband a few years after he was born and
came to live near me in Glastonbury so that I could
help her look after him.

He never learned to speak. He stayed lost in his
own world. But he was happy and contented and had
the most beautiful smile. There was an aura about
him, a glow, that everyone noticed.

Mary and Marie-José took care of Benjamin until, at the
age of fifteen, he slipped away, as peacefully as he had lived.
Though his passing left a huge gap in their lives, they knew
that, for him, it was a release.

'I always felt that he was very special,' Mary said. 'A
beautiful and wise soul trapped inside a damaged body. In
his own way, he gave out so much love.'

It has often been remarked that some children who suffer from Down's Syndrome or other mental or physical dis-
abilities do have a special quality about them. Although they
are not able to develop intellectually like other children they
have happy and sunny dispositions and are full of uncondi-
tional, undemanding love. I am not saying that they are little
angels. Of course they can be mischievous and naughty and
exasperating at times. Looking after them is a demanding
job which requires great sacrifices on the part of their parents. But all the parents I have spoken to have said that all
the sacrifice and the heartache was worth it, for the joy their
children brought into their lives.

Sick Children

The same special qualities can be found in children whose
lives are cut short by sickness and disease. The plight of

such children touches everyone's hearts. No one can fail to be moved when they visit a cancer ward in a children's hospital, seeing the big eyes staring out of pain-filled faces and the bald heads of the children whose hair has fallen out as a result of chemotherapy.

To be told that your child has a terminal illness is every parent's nightmare. Sadly, this happens all too often. Cancer, of which leukaemia is the most common form, is a major cause of childhood deaths, second only to road accidents. Thanks to the advances that have been made in medicine, many cases can now be successfully treated but sometimes, despite the skill and dedication of doctors and nurses, no cure is possible.

The shock of hearing the diagnosis may be just the beginning. The illness can drag on for months or even years, straining the endurance of both parents and child to the limit. Periods of hope, when the disease goes into remission, are followed by despair when there is a relapse. Long stays in hospital may be necessary, with painful treatment which can seem worse than the original disease. And, if the treatment fails, parents can only stand helplessly by, seeing their child grow weaker, knowing that no amount of love can take away the pain or hold back the precious life that is ebbing away.

When a child is diagnosed as terminally ill, the parents are faced with a terrible dilemma. Should they tell the child the seriousness of their condition? Many parents are unable to do this. The truth is so unthinkable that they cannot even face it themselves. They cling to the hope – faint though it may be – of a last-minute reprieve, a miracle. When their child looks them in the eye and asks, 'What is wrong with me? Am I going to get better?' they don't know what to say. They avoid that direct look and try to cheer them up with assurances that they know are false.

Doctors and nurses are equally reluctant to tell young patients the truth. They are in the same dilemma as parents and may, of course, be parents themselves. They do not want to take away the last shred of hope, nor can they bring themselves to tell the child that there is nothing they can do to make them well again.

Dr Melvin Morse, who has worked extensively with dying children, writes about what he calls 'the loving lie'. He claims that, rather than be honest with their patients about their condition, doctors reassure them that they are going to recover or that a new treatment is going to be started. This lie can only be maintained if the patient is kept in ignorance, and therefore, as the disease progresses, doctors become more and more unwilling to answer the patient's questions. Patients collude in this conspiracy of silence. Even if they know that they are more seriously ill than anyone is admitting, they keep their feelings to themselves, knowing that, if they try to discuss them, they will make their relatives and the medical staff uneasy.

Dr Morse remarks, 'Children especially avoid discussing death because they recognise that people visit them less often if they ask questions.' This means that these children are not able to share their fears with anyone or to prepare themselves to take leave of life by saying goodbye to those they love. I am not, of course, saying that children should always be told frankly what the prognosis is. Some young patients would be unable to cope with the truth and there are times when the 'loving lie' is the kindest alternative. But there are occasions when parents and doctors are not so much protecting the child as avoiding facing up to their own fears of death. Did they but realise it, the child may be more aware of the situation than they are.

The American psychiatrist Dr Elisabeth Kübler-Ross, who is famous for her work with the dying, has devoted much of her life to looking after terminally ill children. Unlike so many medical practitioners, she has not been afraid to get involved with her young patients and has taken the time to be with them and listen to them, and this has given her valuable insights into their thoughts and feelings. She believes that children always know instinctively when they are going to die. In *On Children and Death* she writes:

> All children know (not consciously, but intuitively) about the outcome of their illness. All little ones are aware (not on an intellectual, but on a spiritual level) if they are close to death. They will ask occasionally, 'Mom, am I going to die?' Or if they sense that you are unable to talk or even think about it, older children will write a poem or a page in their diary about it. They may confide in a friend or a special person who is not necessarily a member of the family, and thus more able to hear their symbolic language. If they have a roommate in the hospital or a playmate in the hospital playroom, they may share their knowledge with another sick child. Few grownups know how many secrets are shared in such a way.

Her advice to parents is to be honest and not to try to conceal their sadness or put on a mask of false cheerfulness. If they show what they are feeling, the child can confide in them. All the emotion can be brought out into the open and they can comfort each other.

She suggests that the parents should also be honest with the child's brothers and sisters about what is happening. Of course, parents have to judge whether or not it is wise to do this, based on the siblings' age and their ability to understand. But it is better to involve them with the sick child, visiting them in hospital or helping to tend them at home, rather than excluding them in order to spare their feelings. Harrowing though it may be for them, her experience has led her to the conclusion that it is easier for children to come to terms with the death of a sibling if they have been given the opportunity to show their love for their brother or sister while they are alive. This is certainly better than being kept in ignorance, only to be told the dreadful news when it is too late to say goodbye.

Dreams of the Spirit World

As sick children get nearer to the end of their lives, they sometimes become conscious of the spirit world. Children's minds are naturally open and receptive and, as the physical body gets weaker, the inner self comes to the fore. They may have vivid dreams which resemble the visions seen in near-death experiences, of a beautiful land of warmth and sunshine. These are more than mere dreams; the children are taken to the spirit world in their sleep state so as to prepare them for when the time comes for them to enter it. Children need to be able to talk about these dreams and parents should encourage them to do so. One child confided in her father about the place she had seen in a dream, that was so full of love and light that she didn't want to come back. What she remembered most of all, she told him, was that she had met her brother there. The only thing she couldn't understand was that she didn't have a brother. At this, her father burst into tears. He told her that there had been a baby boy who had died three months after she was born, and she had never been told about him.

Dr Morse tells the story of three-year-old Toby, who was in a New York hospital for a check-up. The doctors believed that his leukaemia was in remission but Toby knew otherwise. He told one of the nurses, Rosemarie, about a dream he had had in which he had been taking a trip. Curious, the nurse asked him to draw his dream and he drew a picture that was blue and grey on one side and on the other side had yellow and white flowers, birds and pets:

> 'Pretty soon I am going to a special place,' he said when the drawing was finished. On his way to the special place, Toby said, he would have to pass through a world of darkness, which he pointed to in the left-hand side of his drawing. It wasn't scary though, he told Rosemarie, especially as he knew the beauty that was waiting on the other side.
>
> 'When are you going there?' asked Rosemarie.
>
> 'I don't know for sure,' he told her, 'but it is going to be soon and I'll like it there.'
>
> Within a week Toby died.

Deathbed Visions

Dying children may become aware of spirit visitors who are coming to help them make the transition into the next world. These deathbed visions, as they are known, are well documented in both children and adults. They are nearly always of relatives or friends the person has known and loved. Doctors are well aware of this phenomenon but, predictably, dismiss the visions as hallucinations. However Dr Kübler-Ross is convinced that they are more than this. She points out that a sick child will always want to have its mother by its side and that, if dying children were hallucinating, it would be their mothers that they would see. Yet this does not happen. Their visions are always of people who have died. She says that she has sat by the bedsides of children who were dying, watching over them and holding their hands. She has never known any of them to have visions of living parents.

One child who was injured in a car crash said to her just before his death, 'Everything is all right now. Mommy and Peter are already waiting for me.'

Dr Kübler-Ross was aware that the boy's mother had been killed in the accident but, as far as she knew, his brother Peter, who had been taken to a different hospital, was still alive. But the boy was right. A few minutes later she received a phone call to say that Peter had died ten minutes before.

She writes:

> In thirteen years of studying children near death I have never had one child who has made a single mistake when it comes to identifying – in this way – family members who have preceded them in death.

The End of Treatment

As the illness progresses, parents are faced with another agonising decision. At what stage should they say no to further, possibly painful treatment and think instead of doing all they can to make their child's remaining weeks or days as comfortable and as peaceful as they can?

To decline the treatment is to admit that death is inevitable and this is a heart-breaking admission to have to make. Doctors, who are dedicated to preserving life at all costs, are often keen to try any course of action in order to preserve life a few months or weeks longer, even if there is no quality of life left and no hope of an eventual cure. But there may come a point at which the child himself decides that he does not wish to struggle any longer and may ask to be allowed to go in peace.

Dreams and spirit visions are an indication that this

time is near or has arrived. Some children have waking visions of the spirit world or become suddenly tranquil and at peace. It takes great courage, as well as perception, for parents to recognise these signs and to accept their child's wishes. It is human nature to cling to those we love, especially to our children, and to do everything possible to keep them with us. But sometimes the greatest gift that can be given to a dying child is to release them with love, so that they can set themselves free from the body that has become a prison and enter the world of beauty that is waiting for them.

Olivia's Story

One of the most moving books I have ever read is *Sunday's Child* by Olivia Cox. This is the story of Rebecca, Olivia's daughter, who died of leukaemia at the age of two. Rebecca was one of those special children I have talked about – a gentle, loving child who showed a wisdom beyond her years and seldom complained despite all the pain she had to endure in her short life.

When it became clear that Rebecca did not have long to live, Olivia and her husband Barry decided to let their daughter spend her last days at home with them, rather than having her admitted to hospital. They arranged one last treat for her. Although it was only November, they held Christmas early and invited Rebecca's friend for a party, with Olivia's grandfather dressing up as Father Christmas. Rebecca, in her tinsel crown, was totally absorbed in the fun, but, beneath their smiles, the grown-ups knew that the end was not far off. That night, she developed a cough which rapidly turned into pneumonia. The doctor came, but all he could do was prescribe morphine to relieve the pain.

A few nights later, Olivia was awoken by the disturbed sound of Rebecca's breathing and realised that her daughter was dying. She and Barry held her in their arms as she passed away.

They arranged a simple funeral where no one wore black and encouraged Rebecca's little friends to attend. The chapel was full to overflowing with children, parents and friends. Olivia made a simple daisy chain to put on the small white coffin. Later, they had Rebecca's ashes interred in the botanical gardens, under a cherry tree that had the name 'Pink Perfection'.

Olivia writes of the joy Rebecca brought into her life and of all she learned through both the joy and the pain. Rebecca touched the hearts of all who knew her, not only her family and friends but also the doctors and nurses who looked after her.

One of Olivia's friends wrote:

Her coming to me has helped me immensely to face death; my family's, friends' and my own. It no longer seems so final, so bleak or so empty. She has shown me that the spirit lives on, transcending the limitations of humanity.

Another said:

It took you leaving our world, Becca, to teach me three overwhelming lessons: humility, love, and to let go of my expectations. All hard to do. You may have seemed naive and innocent, but in your smallness and your short time with us, you had more wisdom than I.

Children like this are infinitely precious. Their parents feel privileged to have had the care of them for the few years

they spent on earth. And afterwards, when they look back
over their child's life, they realise how much they themselves
have been changed and softened and opened to the things of
the spirit, by the love their children brought into the world.

Olivia summed up her feelings:

> There is pain in loss, but pain can be the breaking of
> the shell that encloses understanding. And with
> understanding comes healing.

So good does come out of pain and tragedy. But the lives of
these innocent souls pose a question in the mind of every
parent. It is the age-old question to which, seemingly, no
answer can be given. 'Why do little children have to suffer?
If God is good, why does He allow these things to happen?'

9

JOURNEY THROUGH ETERNITY

We live in a world that is full of pain and injustice. Whenever we turn on the television or open a newspaper we are confronted with stories of war, violent death, disease and famine. While our sympathy goes out to all who are afflicted, it is the plight of the children, the innocent victims, that moves us most. We can't help wondering why they should have to suffer. When parents lose a child, this sense of injustice strikes home in a very personal way. 'Why has this happened to me?' they need to know. 'Why my child?'

For those with no religious belief, there never can be any answer to this question. The child's death is just a senseless, random event for which there is no reason or purpose. But those who do believe, or hope, that there is a spiritual dimension to existence are driven to try to find an explanation. Some people discover this within their Christian faith but others turn to the teachings of the East, which offer a perspective on life and death that seems more acceptable to them.

Christians are taught to believe that God is a God of love who looks after all the beings He has created. Parents who have been brought up in this belief find it hard to reconcile it with their loss. They think that God has failed them. He did not answer their desperate prayers or protect the child they entrusted to His care.

They may turn to the Church for help but find little comfort there. The priest or minister will offer what kindness and sympathy he can but, in truth, he is as helpless as they are to provide any explanation. The only advice parents are likely to receive is that God's will is best and they must trust Him – empty words at such a time. It is not surprising that some of them lose their faith altogether.

It is, of course, true that a profound tragedy can awaken spirituality in a person who was not religious before. Being the frail creatures that we are, we go running to God the moment we have a crisis and expect Him to make it better, even though we don't give Him a thought the rest of the time! When people are bereaved, they turn to God because there is no one else to turn to and sometimes, out of the depths of their despair, comes a conviction that not only helps them weather the storm but becomes the motivating force of their lives.

But, if God is all-powerful, why did He not intervene to prevent the tragedy from happening? One possible theory is that, when God created the world, He gave mankind free will to choose between good and evil. Thereafter, He left man to work out his own destiny without interference, as a child has to be allowed to make his own mistakes if he is to learn. Wars, killings and all the suffering and deprivation of the world are caused by man, not God. If man lived in peace and harmony there would be no hatred and intolerance. Nor would there be famine, since the resources of the world would be distributed so that the needs of all were met.

We are all caught up in the stream of life and suffer because of a state of affairs which has not been caused by us as individuals. If a child is killed in a road accident, we cannot blame God. Cars are part of our modern way of life and we enjoy the benefits of them even though we know the potential dangers. If a child contracts a disease, it is not because they or their parents are being punished. Disease is part of the natural environment, though it is becoming increasingly clear that some diseases are caused or aggravated by man-made pollution.

All these things are the consequences of mankind working out his destiny on this planet. God does not interfere in this process. What He does, if we turn to Him, is to give us the strength to cope with whatever we have to face. In life and in death, His love is always with us.

Christian Belief

Christians find inspiration in the life of Jesus, remembering, perhaps, how His mother had to watch Him dying and was powerless to prevent it. For many, Jesus is a living force in the world today. Through prayer, we can feel his presence and draw upon his strength, knowing that He will support us.

Christian parents, however desperately they may wish to cling to their children, know that, if they have to let them go, they are handing them back into the arms of the loving Saviour, who will keep them safe with Him.

In *The Price of Loving*, Jane Davies writes about her little daughter:

> In the days shortly before her death, she would lie curled up in a chair, half dozing, half watching us as we lived out our lives around her. Smiling, she would say, 'I'm so happy. I feel I've got arms tight round me.' Her death was the most exciting moment of my life. Deep in the almost overwhelming pain and grief

of her going I was still conscious of a great joy and triumph; joy that she had not been destroyed by her suffering, that she was still confident and reassured; joy that we were able to hand her back into and onto the greatest Love of all; joy that this was not really the end. I felt a very real sense of a new birth – more painful, but as exciting as her first one seven years earlier. There was an inexplicable but unshakeable knowledge that all was indeed well.

Rabbi Kushner

Whatever faith one follows, prayer, and the belief in God, make it possible to bring something positive out of grief as terrible as that of losing a child. Harold S. Kushner is a Jewish rabbi whose son Aaron was stricken with a dreadful disease called progeria, 'rapid aging'. This meant that he would never grow beyond three feet in height, that he would look like a little old man while he was still a child and that he would die while he was in his early teens.

The rabbi's first, and very natural reaction was anger. He had been a good person and was trying to serve God. How could God do this to him? He wrestled with his doubts for many years while watching his son deteriorate. After Aaron's death he wrote a book, *When Bad Things Happen to Good People*, based on his own experiences and those of the numerous people with whom he had come into contact through his ministry. He concluded:

> I am a more sensitive person, a more effective pastor, a more sympathetic counsellor because of Aaron's life and death than I would ever have been without it. And I would give up all of those gains in a second if

could have my son back. If I could choose, I would forego all the spiritual growth and depth which has come my way because of my experiences, and be what I was fifteen years ago, an average rabbi, an indifferent counsellor, helping some people and unable to help others, and the father of a bright, happy boy. But I cannot choose.

I believe in God. But I do not believe the same things about Him that I did years ago, when I was growing up or when I was a theological student. I recognize His limitations. He is limited in what he can do by laws of nature and by the evolution of human nature and human moral freedom. I no longer hold God responsible for illnesses, accidents, and natural disasters, because I realize that I gain little and lose so much when I blame God for those things. I can worship a God who hates suffering but cannot eliminate it, more easily than I can worship a God who chooses to make children suffer and die, for whatever exalted reason . . . God does not cause our misfortunes. Some are caused by bad luck, some are caused by bad people, and some are simply an inevitable consequence of our being human and being mortal, living in a world of inflexible natural laws. The painful things that happen to us are not punishments for our misbehaviour, nor are they in any way part of some grand design on God's part. Because the tragedy is not God's will, we need not feel hurt or betrayed by God when tragedy strikes. We can turn to Him for help in overcoming it, precisely because we can tell ourselves that God is as outraged by it as we are.

Rabbi Kushner's words will strike a chord with many parents, who would agree that they are better, more sympathetic people because of what they have been through, and are therefore able to help others. But they might well argue that the loss of their child was too high a price to pay for anything they may have learned or gained. Life does present us with some bitter lessons. Perhaps what matters in the end is the way we react to them, whether we let ourselves become angry and embittered or whether we accept them as part of the learning process. If we can accept them, then they become, as Olivia Cox wrote, 'the breaking of the shell that encloses understanding'. As that shell breaks, so the healing power of God can flow into our lives.

Mary Clifford's Story

I have already mentioned Mary Clifford's two daughters, Sheila and Gillian, both of whom died before they reached the age of twenty. This is Mary's story:

> Sheila was born in 1952. She was a healthy child until the age of eight, when she began to suffer from epileptic fits. She was taken to Great Ormond Street hospital where we were told she had a brain disease, neurolippidosis or cerebral muscular degeneration. This disease is very rare. It can affect boys or girls but it nearly always strikes in childhood up to the age of twelve. It affects vision and speech and the coordination of the limbs.
>
> The Great Ormond Street specialist told us, 'Imagine all the nerves in the brain being bunched together and fastened with insulating tape. In this illness, the insulating tape gradually disintegrates and the first thing that happens is epilepsy and loss of vision.' We were told that there was no cure and

warned that, as time went on, Sheila would become more and more disabled. They didn't give her long to live.

Needless to say, my husband Peter and I were shattered. The doctor who told us cried with us. At first we found it very hard to take it in. Sheila was sent to Carshalton Hospital in Surrey where they had a form of schooling on the wards. She gradually deteriorated, as we had been warned she would. We had to watch her slowly getting worse. She lost her sight and coordination and spent the last two years of her life in a wheelchair. Then her speech went as well. She finally died two weeks before her fifteenth birthday.

Our second daughter, Gillian, was nine when Sheila was diagnosed. She had to watch her sister suffering and knew all about the trauma we went through. But at least she seemed healthy and we were assured that the disease very rarely strikes twice in the same family. Then, when she was eleven and a half, she developed epilepsy. That was the worst part, knowing we were going to lose her as well.

Gillian's deterioration was more gradual than Sheila's but, like Sheila, she also lost her sight. She was sent to a special school for children who were blind and had additional handicaps. She coped wonderfully well with her disability. She learned braille and won a bronze award for swimming, learned roller skating and rode ponies. Later, she went to a senior school but at the age of fourteen they had to discharge her because her brain's capacity for learning had ceased. So she was sent to the same hospital as Sheila and managed to get herself onto the same ward, where she was looked after by the same nurse who had taken care of Sheila.

By that time she, like Sheila, was in a wheelchair. She stayed at the hospital until she died, just after her nineteenth birthday.

Like all parents in our situation, we wondered why this disaster should have happened to us. We asked all the usual questions: Where is the love of God? What have we done wrong? You don't ever recover from a thing like this but gradually wisdom and the experience of the years takes over. I've come to see that this was something my husband and I had to go through so that we could help other people. I had been interested in Spiritualism when my daughters were alive but after they died I got more involved and became a medium myself. I meet many parents with handicapped children or who have lost children in various ways and know exactly what they are going through because I have been there myself.

My belief in reincarnation has also helped me. I think our daughters chose to go through those illnesses because of something they needed to learn. They chose us as parents because they knew we could give them what they needed, both the medical help and the spiritual understanding.

Reincarnation

For Mary and Peter, as for many other parents who have come through their bereavement to find new meaning in their lives, the belief that we incarnate many times on earth offers some solution to the eternal problem of suffering. Reincarnation is a major tenet of Hinduism and Buddhism and is now becoming increasingly accepted in the West. This doctrine claims that we are all spiritual beings travelling on a journey through eternity. We were originally created by God like children, in a state of innocence, and we existed in a spiritual dimension far removed from the earth. However, in order to develop, we had to move away from this state of innocence, as a child needs to leave its parents' side in order to grow up.

Gradually, we descended through the planes until we reached the earth. This is the lowest plane, the point furthest removed from heaven. It is like a school where we come to learn the lessons of right and wrong, good and evil. We come here countless times because there is so much we have to learn. Our incarnations take us to every part of the world. We live sometimes as a man, sometimes as a woman. We experience every conceivable aspect of the human condition – riches and poverty, hunger and plenty, fame and obscurity. In the course of our existence we undergo much pain and suffering but this is all part of our development. The law of karma, or cause and effect, which is closely linked with that of reincarnation, teaches that we are responsible for our own progress. If we do something wrong in one lifetime, we will have to atone for it at some future time.

However, karma should not be thought of as a system of rewards and punishments. It would be better to see it as a learning process. The soul is like a jewel. It has to be ground and polished before its true beauty can be revealed. The whole purpose of our existence on earth is to develop our inner self so that, by loving and serving others, we can polish the jewel of our soul and continue our spiritual evolution.

But, however many times we come to earth, the spirit world remains our soul's true home and we return there after each lifetime. Eventually, when we have learned all we can from this plane of existence, we go back there for good. We then ascend gradually back up through the astral plane and the higher dimensions until, finally, we reach heaven, and so the circle is complete.

Choosing Our Parents

According to the doctrine of reincarnation, many of the people we meet on our journey through life, our families, partners and friends, are people we have known in past lives. We encounter the same souls again and again, though the relationship may be different. For instance, your son in this life may have been your father, mother, brother or friend in a former time. Usually, it is bonds of love that draw us together, but not always. One of the ways in which karma teaches us is to place us in situations where we encounter old enemies, so as to give us the opportunity to transmute the bitterness of the past into love.

We choose our parents. Many mothers-to-be instinctively sense this. They state with confidence, long before the birth, whether the child they are carrying is a boy or a girl. They may have vivid dreams about the soul that is coming and will be able to say in advance what their character will be like. Sometimes, they feel prompted to give the child a particular name which may not be a name they would have selected themselves.

The soul that is waiting to be born hovers around the mother from the time of conception until the birth. There is considerable debate about the exact point at which the soul joins the foetus. Some say that it is at the moment of conception, others that it is at the quickening (when the baby begins to kick in the womb). This is a complex subject and one I do not have space to explore in detail here, but my own feeling is that it is a gradual process. The soul blends itself with the baby growing in the womb until, by the time of the birth, it is fully integrated into the new body.

Being Born

We are told by the spirit world that being born is far more unpleasant than dying. The soul has to leave the freedom of the astral plan and descend into a world that seems grey and drab, where it knows it will have to undergo many trials and hardships. The physical body feels heavy after the lightness of the astral form.

Many souls are reluctant to come and only do so because they know that the particular family and circumstances they have chosen will provide the conditions for them to make spiritual progress. These reluctant souls are quiet and withdrawn as babies. Gentle by nature, they spend long periods of time lost in their own dreams, recalling, perhaps, the world they have left behind. Lively, extrovert children, on the other hand, are souls who have come to earth eagerly. They cannot wait to get started on the adventure of a new life!

The parents know nothing of the baby's inner life. They fondly imagine that the child's mind is a blank book, waiting to be filled. In fact, many of the pages are already written. The new life is merely a new chapter. Of course, the parents will greatly influence, for good or ill, the way in which this new chapter is written but the soul has its own agenda to follow and, whatever they do, will work out its own destiny.

Handicapped Children

Children who are handicapped, or who suffer serious illness or disease, are souls who have come to earth to master very difficult lessons. It may seem incomprehensible that a soul would deliberately choose a damaged body, but we cannot judge, with our earthly understanding, the motives of the eternal being within. Often, these children are advanced souls who have lived on earth many times and finished nearly all the lessons they had to learn. They are here for one last life, to complete their round of earthly incarnations, after which they will never need to incarnate again. It is the soul within, and the wisdom they have gathered in all these past lives, that gives these children the spiritual quality so many of them possess.

Part of their mission in coming to the world is to stir the souls of their parents, families and all those with whom they come into contact, to help them to find the spirit within themselves. This may seem a hard teaching, especially to parents who have just lost their child and who can think of nothing but the pain they are feeling. But it is a concept that some parents do eventually accept and find comforting because it gives their children's lives a special purpose.

Mary told me that she sensed from the beginning that Benjamin had come for a reason, and this helped to reconcile her to his handicap:

When we first discovered how badly handicapped he was I was very sad but, even then, I had a feeling that a divine plan was being worked out. I didn't always find it easy to keep sight of this knowledge when my daughter and I were struggling to bring him up but I knew this plan was a two-way process. He was learning whatever he came here to learn but he was teaching us at the same time. My daughter become very interested in reincarnation and other spiritual teachings and my own spiritual understanding was deepened.

Since he passed into the spirit world, both Marie-José and I have had dreams which were more than dreams, in which we have seen him as a young man, perfect in body and mind. He achieved whatever he came to do and he is happy in spirit now.

Accident or Design?

Reincarnation offers an explanation as to why some children have such short lives. They have lived on earth many times before and only needed to come for a little while, in order to undergo a particular experience or complete a specific task. Once that is done, they return to spirit. From our point of view, it appears that their life was taken away when they had everything to live for, but from their standpoint, it was the right time for them to leave. Time has no meaning for the soul and, whether we live on earth for eight or eighty years, it is only an infinitesimal part of our eternal journey.

What appears to be a freak accident may have been part of their soul's plan. In many cases, children who have died suddenly, in a road accident, for example, seem in their inner selves to have been prepared for what was to come. Their parents describe them as being unusually mature and living life to the full. One father said of his son, 'He packed more living into those few years than most people do in a life-time.' It is as though they are aware, at some subliminal level, that they will not be here long. When they come back through mediums, they confirm that they did have some inner warning but they say they have been taught, since their arrival in the spirit world, that it was their time to go. They are completely without bitterness and their only regret is the sorrow they have caused their families.

Michael and June Cowlin received a long series of communications from their son Peter, which June recorded in *Truth is Veiled*. Peter had been travelling on his motorbike along a familiar, straight stretch of road late one night when he failed to remember a minor road junction. He saw, too late, the traffic lights at red and, unable to stop in time, hit the rear of a car crossing his path.

Peter's parents were rung by the police in the early hours of the morning. They told them that their son had been involved in a motorcycle accident and taken to hospital. Michael and June rushed to the hospital, where Peter was lying unconscious. Tests showed, however, that his life was not in danger. A few days later, he was out of intensive care and appeared to be doing well. The medical team were satisfied with his progress. But Peter seemed quiet and pre-occupied and would sometimes smile as if in response to con-versation with people no one else could see. Suddenly one day his temperature shot up. Within a few hours he was dead.

But Peter's parents were convinced that he was not far away. Michael, who had developed the ability to hear spirits some years before, heard Peter speak to him on a number of occasions. Aware that Peter had more he wanted to say to them, they formed a group with a family friend who was a medium. Over the next few years, Peter spoke to them regu-larly, telling them about his life in the spirit world and about what he had learned there.

He told his parents that they had been with him in the spirit world before their birth and that they had chosen to come back together. It was agreed that Peter would have a short life. At a subconscious level, he had been aware of this plan: 'I felt a great need to enjoy all the earth had to offer because, from my inner being, I knew my spell on earth would be short.'

The inquest brought in a verdict of accidental death but he knew differently:

I think it was much more direct than that! They tell me here that very little is the result of chance. Most things are either the result of Karma, or the result of a plan of living, or the person's free will. I think I would have died about this time anyhow, from some cause if not the motorcycle. As you know, I sort of had a feeling about this.

He explained how his life as Peter fitted into the whole pattern of his existence and summed up what he had been taught in the spirit world about reincarnation:

I think I have a totally different vision of life now, as just one episode in a continuing serial of existence, which consists of many Earth lives linked by periods in the worlds I am in now. No, that's badly put. It's really the other way round. The continuing stream of life takes place where I am now.

But here one need not extend oneself at all. One can just live an infinitely easy life only too readily. So periods on Earth are to give one the difficult experiences to balance up.

It's like being on a cruise ship. Most of the time one lounges in a deck chair in the sun, with every comfort. But sometimes one enters a foreign port, and goes ashore to meet difficulties, speak a foreign language, and work through foreign customs. By the time one re-embarks, one is quite glad to be back in the familiar comfort of the ship, until another foreign port is reached.

But one looks back on the experience of being ashore – how one got on with the natives – and can recount tales of one's adventures. One learns from one's experiences. I'm well re-embarked at present, no other port in sight!

Will We Meet Again?

Reincarnation is just one possible answer to the mystery of why there is so much suffering. It is not an answer that every parent will find acceptable. No one can fully understand the purpose of our lives or see the plan behind existence. But the teachings of all religions, and our own inner knowledge, tell us that there is a divine plan. Our lives are a tapestry in which dark and light threads are interwoven. While we are on earth, we cannot make sense of the pattern but when we get to the spirit world we will be able to stand back and see how the dark threads gave the design its depth and beauty.

Before leaving the topic of reincarnation, there is one last point I must deal with, because it is something that troubles many parents who hold this philosophy. As one mother put it to me: 'If we do come back, will I see my son again or will he have returned to earth by the time I get there?'

I can only say that, in my experience as a medium, I have had many children come back through me, and I have never been told by my spirit helpers that a particular child could not be contacted because he had reincarnated. Souls may remain in the spirit world for a long time between lives; maybe hundreds of years of our time. I have mentioned that miscarried children sometimes return to earth fairly quickly but this is not invariably the case; often they stay in the spirit world and grow up there. The very spiritual children who come to earth as our teachers will not need to return to earth again.

But reincarnation, as I understand it, is not just the same person coming back again and again. We all have within us a higher self. This is the innermost part of our being and, like our own personal guardian angel, it oversees the course of our whole existence. This higher self never incarnates in its entirety. It puts forth one part of itself, one facet, in each lifetime. This facet forms the basis of the personality we have in that life, which will then be developed by the experiences we undergo. When we die, that personality lives on into the spirit world and develops further there, even though it is possible that the higher self may send down another facet of itself to incarnate on earth.

These are profound mysteries upon which man has always speculated. Even the teachers who speak to us from the next world do not always agree about the workings of destiny. They are, however, unanimous in saying that the universe is ruled by love and that, whether we live on earth only once or return here many times, where there is a deep spiritual bond between one soul and another, that bond will always draw them back together, because it is stronger than death.

10

WHAT SHALL WE TELL THE CHILDREN?

So far I have spoken of the grief of parents on losing a child but there is another group of people who need just as much consideration: the brothers and sisters who are left behind.

Children have been called the forgotten mourners. When a young person dies, the sympathy of the family and friends is concentrated on the bereaved parents. Because the children are young, it is assumed that they are not so deeply affected. In fact, children suffer just as much as adults but, because they may not be able to express their feelings clearly, their needs are frequently overlooked.

A Child's First Encounter with Death

Fifty or a hundred years ago, children were conditioned to accept death as part of the human lot. 'In the midst of life we are in death,' the preachers warned. Life expectancy was shorter than it is today. Diseases such as tuberculosis and diphtheria were rife. Few children reached adulthood unscathed by the loss of a sibling, parent or someone they held dear.

Today, the situation is very different. The modern child may never encounter death, unless it be the death of a grandparent. This, of course, can be deeply upsetting. A grandparent may be a surrogate parent and confidante, as well as an indulgent provider of sweets and presents. The child may not understand what has happened or why grand-dad doesn't come and see him any more. 'Where has grand-dad gone?' he wants to know. 'He's gone to heaven,' he is told, but no one explains where heaven is.

The death of a beloved pet also cuts deep with a child, for whom the animal may have been their closest companion. 'He'll soon get over it,' parents tell themselves, as they bury the little body in the garden. They buy the child a new cat, dog or rabbit and, sure enough, he quickly becomes as devoted to that as he was to the animal who died. But a shadow has been cast over his mind of which the adults are completely unaware and his world will never seem quite so safe and secure again.

When a Parent Dies

If a parent dies, the child is thrown into emotional turmoil. His whole world is shattered. He may feel rejected and abandoned; he may fear that the other parent will leave him as well and he may blame himself.

June, who is now in her thirties, spoke to me about the death of her father:

I was four when my father was killed in an accident. I can't remember much about it. My mother tells me that I just shut off completely. I never even mentioned his name. It was so overwhelming that I couldn't talk about it. I thought it was my fault and that he had gone away because he didn't love me. No one really explained what had happened. My mother didn't cry in front of me so I didn't feel that I could cry either. Because of that, I never mourned him properly.

Children in this sad situation need a lot of demonstrative love. If the remaining parent is too grief-stricken to provide this, and there is no other adult they can turn to who can to some extent take the place of the parent who has died, they are left with emotional scars that may never heal.

When a Sibling Dies

It is every parent's natural instinct to shield their child from the pain of death. If a child is sick or dying, they often withhold this information from the other children in order to spare them the pain. But if the children are not warned, then the death, when it occurs, causes an even greater trauma. One girl wrote to me:

I was seven when my little sister died. She was in hospital and had a heart condition but nobody told me how serious it was, so it was a complete shock. I was angry at my parents for not warning me. At least then I would have had the chance to say goodbye and to tell her I loved her. I only hope she knows now.

To lose a sibling, in whatever way, is an experience that a child never forgets and, in many cases, never gets over. This can be a very lonely time, especially if the death means that they then become an only child. They have no one left to play with or share their secrets with. The parents may be too wrapped up in their own grief to have time for them. People ask, 'How is your mother?' or 'How is your father coping?' No one thinks to ask how they are coping. They feel isolated and in the way.

But they have to keep these feelings bottled up inside. Most adults, like June's mother, are careful not to let the children see their grief. Children are acutely sensitive to emotional undercurrents but, because their parents are not being open with them, they feel that they have to put on a brave face. Little boys, especially, believe that they must be brave and not cry. As Elisabeth Kübler-Ross advises, it is better if parents let the children see their sadness, rather than putting on a mask of false cheerfulness. The children can then share their emotions and they can comfort each other.

Adults often torment themselves with guilt when a child dies, reproaching themselves for not having been sufficiently loving and regretting any harsh words that have been spoken. They do not realise that children can feel just as guilty as they think back to times when they were impatient with their brother or sister or unkind to them – which siblings don't squabble occasionally? Unlike adults, they are unable to rationalise these feelings and their guilt becomes a secret and quite unnecessary burden – 'My brother got run over because I shouted at him' or 'my sister died because I was jealous of her.'

The whole range of emotions experienced by grieving adults is felt by children as well. All these emotions need to be shared and lived through as a family. The family that grieves together, heals together.

Funeral Rites

The rituals with which we surround death can be very puzzling to a child. A friend gave me a typical example of how children are confused:

> When I was very young, there were two elderly sisters who lived in the house down the road. I knew that one of them had died and I saw the procession of cars leaving for her funeral. But I couldn't for the life of me work out what was in the big box in the car in front.

I remember several family funerals when I was a child. The adults would be wearing black, talking in hushed voices about some relative of whom I had never heard. They would then go off to the funeral where, apparently, everyone was expected to cry. But I couldn't understand why, if it was so sad, they then came back to the house for sherry and cake and had such a jolly time!

The thought of burying someone in a grave is enough to give a sensitive child nightmares. 'Why are they putting Granny in the ground? Will she be able to breathe down there?' The idea of cremation is even more frightening.

The euphemisms which adults use to avoid mentioning death can also be confusing. To say that someone has 'gone to sleep' makes a child afraid to go to sleep himself in case he never wakes up. I was puzzled when I was told that my aunt had 'lost' her husband. I wondered how she had been so careless as to mislay him and whether she would find him in the lost property office!

Parents need to be very careful about the expressions they use, and consider how these can be misinterpreted by the young and impressionable. They should take time to explain, in words the child can understand, what happens to the body when someone dies and that it is no longer the person themselves but just the empty shell that is left behind.

Attending the Funeral

Children are often not allowed to attend funerals because their parents think it will upset them. However, counsellors and those who deal with bereaved children now consider that a child should be permitted to go to the funeral of someone he has loved and that, if he is not permitted to do so, he may well regret it in later years.

In the case of a child's funeral, the siblings should be allowed to attend if they wish. Of course, no child should be forced to go if they don't want to, but most children, given the opportunity, would prefer to be there. It is a good idea to involve them actively in the service, by letting them choose the music or read a poem. They may also like to place some small memento in the coffin, as their own personal tribute to the brother or sister who has died.

Children's Awareness of the Spirit World

It is, as I have said, common for parents to sense the closeness of a child who has died. Children are just as likely to experience this. They are more open to the spirit world than adults because they have only recently left that world to come to earth. The rational level of mind, which tends to block out psychic awareness, has not developed in them yet, so they are receptive to impressions that come from the

Beyond. A child who is psychic will accept the presence of spirit visitors in a calm, matter-of-fact way and will quite happily tell you, for instance, that Granny sits on the end of his bed at night talking to him. Parents often find this ability disconcerting.

Margaret French's parents received a shock when she told them about the spirit children who visited her at night:

Being an only child I always felt sad to see other children with brothers and sisters – but always felt that I had brothers and sisters, a fact which, when I tackled my mother and father about it, was always hotly denied.

One night, I was awakened by a kind of tinkly music and three children were standing at the side of my bed. I remember sitting up and thinking how beautiful they were, all dressed in shining gold that sparkled. They started talking to me and said that they were my brothers and sister and that their names were Roger, John and Margaret. They had all been born at the same time but had not been on earth very long. After a few minutes they disappeared.

In the morning, I told Mum and Dad what I had seen and the names of the three children, who were about two years older than myself. I was surprised to be accused of going through their private papers, which I hotly denied. Eventually, after standing my ground, they gave in and told me that my mother had had triplets who had lived just long enough to be baptised. We lived in Oxford at that time and I was taken to see the grave in St Clement's churchyard. I have never forgotten the beauty and love I felt whilst talking to them.

The imaginary playmates some children have may, in fact, be spirits. Children are convinced that these little playmates are real and may insist that their parents provide toys for them or lay an extra place for them at the table. Strangely, they never seem to question where their little friends come from or wonder why they may not be dressed like normal children.

Ann told me about the little boy she and her sister Edie used to see:

> When Edie and I were both under five, we had a little friend called Billy we used to play with. He was just an ordinary boy, dressed in modern clothes. We both saw him and didn't think there was anything strange about it. I would say to Edie, 'Shall we play with Billy today?' and he would just be there. He was quite real and solid. We never heard him speak – we spoke to him in our minds. We never saw him leave or knew where he went but suddenly he would be gone. Our parents knew about him and accepted him. At about the age when we started to go to school he stopped coming and we didn't see him again.

Memories of the Spirit World

Some children carry with them the consciousness of the place they were in before they came to earth. Beryl's little grandson George was five when he startled her one day by saying, 'Granny, I remember before I was born.'

'Do you, dear?' Beryl asked, trying not to sound too surprised.

'I was in the sky,' George went on quite casually. 'I looked down and saw Mummy and Daddy and decided I liked them and that I would be born to them.'

George also told his father Andrew about being 'in the sky'.

'We were talking about what he had been doing at school that day,' Andrew told me:

> He stopped talking for a moment and went very
> serious and then he said, 'Daddy, before I came here
> I could see everything.' I asked him what he meant.
> He said he could see the world and everything in it
> but since he'd been born he was no longer able to see
> everything. He could see certain things, like his
> mother and me at work. And he went on to describe
> what we do.
>   Then he said, 'Before I was born I flied down and
> visited you and Mummy and decided I liked you so I
> was born. But I still go and see God and Jesus and
> we talk. I don't mind not seeing so much because I
> do like it here.'

Children like George display an unusual maturity. They are often called 'old souls' because there is a look in their eyes that suggests they have been here many times before. Andrew says that his little boy often 'blows his mind' with his wisdom and the love he has for others.

Psychic Children

When I was a child, I had many psychic experiences which I kept to myself because I knew that no one in the family would understand them. I never saw spirits but I sensed invisible presences around me and sometimes heard them speaking to me inside my head. Because I couldn't talk to anyone about this, I wasn't sure whether it was real or whether I had an over-active imagination. Although my family was loving, I often felt different, as though I didn't belong there.

I was acutely sensitive to any telling-off or criticism and was mortified if anyone laughed at me. I used to have premonitions, mainly about trivial things, but they invariably came true. I was very shy and would run away and hide when visitors came, unless they were people I knew well. As we had a large house, my embarrassed parents were usually unable to find me and were extremely annoyed with me when I emerged from my hiding place after the guests had left. I was also very sensitive to the atmospheres of places. I remember once being taken to visit a ruined castle and refusing point-blank to go up the spiral staircase in the tower to see the view. I knew there was something evil in that tower and no amount of coaxing, not even the promise of an ice-cream, would persuade me to go up there!

As I got older, I gave little indication of any psychic awareness. This was not because it left me but because I had learned that people were uncomfortable if I spoke about it. No child likes to be thought odd. When, in later years, I was able to discuss my childhood experiences with other people who were psychic, I discovered that they had all had similar experiences.

If Your Child is Psychic

Psychic children can be difficult for parents to handle. Not that they are troublesome – on the contrary, they tend to be good-natured and anxious to please. But they are highly sensitive and need a lot of love and understanding. They also need to be protected from the harsh realities of life.

They cannot defend themselves in the rough and tumble of the playground and may be bullied by the other children. Children can be cruel and are apt to pick on a child who, for whatever reason, doesn't seem to fit in.

If you have a child who is psychic, be especially patient and gentle with him. These delicate souls need special care. Encourage him to share his feelings, impressions and dreams with you but don't always expect him to explain – he probably doesn't understand them himself! Reassure him that there is nothing weird about him. Don't suggest that he is making things up. If you offend him, he will retreat into his shell. Above all, don't laugh at him or he will never confide in you again.

Accept that your child is aware of spirit people, even if you are not aware of them yourself. If he has a brother or sister in the spirit world and says that he sees them or that they speak to him, do not brush it aside or tell him that he is imagining it. Tell him that they are looking after him. Do not react with fear or you will make him fearful. Show him that his ability is something natural, which indeed it is. If you do this, he will learn to value and respect his own sensitivity.

In most psychic children, the psychic ability diminishes as they grow up. This is partly because they become absorbed in the life around them but also because they unconsciously suppress it, as they realise that it is considered unacceptable. In doing this, they lose their connection with the spirit world. There are, on the other hand, a few children who retain this connection and show a potential for mediumship. Although this is a wonderful gift to have, I personally would not advise any parent to let their child work seriously on developing this potential unless the child is determined to do so and is very mature. It is hard enough for teenagers and young people today to cope with the pressures of growing up in this world, without taking on the added responsibility of being a channel of communication for the next! I believe that it is best for them to let the gift unfold naturally at its own pace until they grow up, and they can then decide if this is the work they want to do.

Children's Attitudes to Death

Because they are so reluctant to talk to children about death, adults have little idea of their thoughts and feelings on the subject. They usually assume that children don't think about death at all. In fact, children are immensely curious about it. They are also sometimes very frightened, particularly if someone they know has died.

Ann, who now has three children of her own, told me about her fear and how it was overcome:

When I was seven or eight, I was obsessed with death and very frightened of it. One night, I had a dream. I was taken to a place I was told was called the Golden Land. I didn't see the person who took me there but it was the most beautiful place I had ever seen. The meadows, the trees were so fresh and green. The colours of the flowers were more vivid than anything on earth. The water was sparkling and clear. It was all absolutely perfect.

I desperately wanted to stay there but the person beside me said, 'You have to go back now, but one day you can come back here again'. I woke up feeling completely peaceful and relaxed. And I was never afraid of death again because I knew that, when I did die, that was the place I was going to.

A friend of mine, Jean, who is a schoolteacher, recently conducted a mini-survey among her class of eleven- to thirteen-year-olds in which she asked them their views on death. The results were instructive. None of these children had lost a sibling but several had lost grandparents. Most said that they were afraid of death and tried not to think about it. Nearly all of them had been taught the traditional doctrine of heaven and hell.

One child wrote: 'My parents have told me that, unless I become a Christian, I will go to hell.' I wonder if they have stopped to consider what fear they are instilling in that child's mind?

Awin wrote: 'I think after you are dead you are gone from earth and you stay somewhere else, maybe not heaven and maybe not hell.'

Quite a few believed in ghosts and spirits. Katie wrote about the spirit she felt in her house but added: 'It's no good trying to tell my parents this because they'll think I'm stupid.'

A couple of children mentioned reincarnation. My favourite comment came from Danny: 'I think it would be pretty cool to die because you would be with millions of famous legends like Hendrix and Marilyn Monroe. I think when you die you stay in heaven where it's really cool for about fifty years, then you get reincarnated back to earth as a human.'

Several children had a conception of the Afterlife as a different dimension. Darryl had it pretty well worked out: 'I think ghosts are people but in a different dimension. Sometimes the dimension breaks and for a second you see a shadow or a person.'

But he seemed to think that they came from the Bermuda Triangle!

Explaining Death to Children

Most parents are at a loss as to how to explain death to their children. Children like George, who remembered being in the spirit world, present little problem. They already understand death better than their parents do. But what do you say to the average child?

If you have strong religious views, you will no doubt wish to share these with them, but if you are not sure what you believe, it is better to admit it. Children respect honesty and have an uncanny knack of knowing when they are being fobbed off with glib explanations. Telling a child that someone has gone to heaven, when you don't believe this yourself, will only confuse them.

Should you sense that the person who has died is still close, let your child know this. They may well sense the presence too and, if they are at all frightened, you can tell them that spirits cannot do them any harm and that they only come back to give love and comfort.

There is no reason why, if you are attending a Spiritualist church, you should not take your child with you, provided that they are not likely to be bored and disruptive to other members of the congregation. Churches are pleased to welcome young people. When children reach their teens they are old enough to make up their own minds what they believe. Many teenagers these days are keenly interested in all aspects of the spiritual and psychic. Hymns and prayers may not be their cup of tea, but they often welcome the opportunity to explore ideas about the Afterlife and to make their own investigations.

Parents who are personally convinced of the existence of the spirit world have no trouble in explaining it to their children. The idea of hell is terrifying to a child (or an adult) and the traditional view of heaven isn't very enticing or very plausible. But even young children will happily accept the idea of a beautiful world where everything is peace and harmony and where they can be with people they love. If they are old enough, they can be given books to read which describe the spirit world or which contain accounts of near-death experiences, which show us that death is not to be feared.

It is more difficult to explain to a child why their brother or sister should have died. Children ask the same questions as adults – 'Why did it have to happen?' 'Wasn't God looking after them?' Some of the ideas I have suggested in this book, which may provide a reasoned explanation for adults, are too complicated to put across to a young child. Perhaps the best that can be said is that their brother or sister has gone to somewhere where they are happy, but that they still love them and are watching over them.

Children have their own way of coming to terms with death. Little William, who had lost his older brother Oliver, was inconsolable until he decided that he knew where Oliver had gone. His mother told me:

> One night I was putting him to bed and went to pull the curtains, as I always do. William said to me, 'Don't pull the curtains, Mummy.'
> 'Why not, dear?' I asked him.
> 'Because Oliver's up there.' He pointed to the sky. 'You see all the stars? Well, he's the brightest star.'
> Now, whenever I look up at the stars, I think of Oliver.

Don't be afraid to talk to your children about death. Let them know what you think and listen to them as well. They might just teach you a thing or two!

11

TO LIVE AGAIN

Grief can be all-consuming. When a child dies, the parents feel that their own lives have ended also. Nothing seems to have meaning any more. They are convinced that they will never be able to smile, laugh or enjoy themselves again.

The road to recovery is long and slow. No one can hurry you or tell you how long it should take. In a sense, there is no recovery from a blow as devastating as this. As so many parents have told me, all you can do is to learn to accommodate it. But there are many milestones along the way and each one you pass is a little victory over despair. There is the first time you are able to laugh at a joke or take pleasure in the beauty of a flower. For a woman, the first time you feel strong enough to visit the hairdresser or go shopping and buy yourself a new outfit is a major achievement. Perhaps one of the most important milestones along the road is when you can see other mothers with their children without feeling unbearable pangs of envy.

The periods of depression are still there. There are times when waves of pain sweep over you, as intense as ever. But the depression does recede. Gradually, the waves become shallower, further apart. You forget about your grief for just a few minutes, then for a couple of hours or perhaps a whole morning. That is not to say that you forget your child – as if you could ever do that! But you are able to immerse yourself in some activity, probably something ordinary like reading a book or digging the garden, and for a while the heaviness leaves you. Then you begin to realise that, impossible though it once seemed, you can start to live again.

Now, at last, you can talk about your child without wanting to burst into tears. You can laugh, as you share with friends and family some happy reminiscences and talk about those things you loved about them, even those things which infuriated you, and which you would give the world to have back again now. What you must not do, as this gradual process of recovery begins, is to feel guilty. You are not being disloyal to your child's memory. The last thing they would want is for you to prolong your grief or to shut yourself away from all the good things that life still has to offer you.

Some parents remain permanently locked in anger and bitterness. It is hard to forgive fate for depriving you of what you held most dear, even harder to forgive if the death was the result of someone else's negligence or carelessness – for instance, in a road accident. The children themselves are able to forgive and may even be taught that it was their time to go. It is very difficult for parents to accept this but, if they can do so, this acceptance can bring healing.

Maureen, whose twenty-year-old son Matthew was killed in a road accident on his way to work, spoke of her feelings:

> At the inquest, I saw the boy who had been driving the car that killed Matthew. The boy's uncle was with him. He said the boy was so very, very sorry and that he had been ill himself since. I felt I had to say to

him, 'I forgive you and know Matthew forgives you too and wants you to get on with your life.' Hatred is very destructive.

The parents who have most cause to be bitter are those whose child was murdered. We all feel shock and revulsion when we hear media reports of the horrific crimes that are committed against children, crimes which now seem to be more frequent. Even if the criminal is caught and sent to prison, no punishment is adequate. It is the parents who bear the life sentence and who will never forget the nightmare. Only the most exceptional of parents, those with a deep faith in God and love for others, can find it in their hearts to forgive under such circumstances. But these people are a shining light to us all and prove that the human spirit is strong enough to rise above any catastrophe.

Colin Caffell went through almost unbelievable trauma when his two small children, Daniel and Nicholas, were murdered. He tells his very moving story in his book *In Search of the Rainbow's End*. The Bamber murders, as they were called in the press, attracted great media interest and his agony was made worse by the unwelcome attention of reporters seeking to uncover lurid details. At first it seemed that the murders were committed by Colin's ex-wife, Sheila, who was also thought to have murdered her adopted parents before turning the gun on herself. Later, it emerged that all the killings had been carried out by Sheila's brother, Jeremy Bamber.

Colin somehow managed to deal with the pain, by working on himself, through a long voyage of self-discovery. He came to the realisation that part of the purpose of his sons' lives had been to lead him to make this search. He now gives workshops and has a private practice, helping and counselling other victims of bereavement and trauma.

Loving is Letting Go

One mother I know of keeps her son's room exactly as it was on the night when he went out and got run over. His clothes are still on the bed, the cassette he had been listening to is still in the CD player. The room feels as if he might walk back in at any moment. This woman's other children loved their brother but they are becoming resentful. In a sense, they have lost their mother as well, since she is so wrapped up in her own emotions and no longer has time for them.

My heart goes out to this woman and to others like her. In their attempts to make time stand still, to preserve every little memory, they are harming themselves and being unfair to those on earth who still need their love. They are also harming their children in spirit. Excessive grief like this holds a child back. Although they are in a more beautiful world, they sense their parents' sorrow. This makes them sad and they feel compelled to stay close to their parents, doing what they can to comfort them. Unfortunately, there is little they can do, since it is very difficult to get through to people whose minds are clouded with depression.

Children do understand that their parents miss them. They miss their parents at first – there is a need for adjustment on both sides. They appreciate your need to cry. There is no point in suppressing your emotions, since, in any case, they can read your thoughts! But if you can recognise, through your tears, that they are well and being cared for and that it is the physical presence that you are missing, then you will not be causing them distress or preventing them from progressing.

If your child went to live in another country where his prospects were better, you would obviously miss him. When he first got there you would write to him or ring him often to find out if he was all right. But once you knew that he was happy, although you would still keep in touch, you wouldn't expect to have such frequent contact. It is the same when a child goes into the spirit world. At first, you will be anxious about his wellbeing and you will want to hear from him as often as possible. But if, when you are convinced that he has survived death and is happy where he is, you keep trying to contact him all the time, you will make it hard for him to settle – it is as if you were constantly calling him to the phone!

By all means, have sittings with mediums from time to time. Your child will welcome this opportunity to let you know how he is getting on. Accept him with love whenever he comes to you, and know that he is watching over you. But don't cling to him. There is a saying: 'If you love something, let it go and it will return to you.' Set your child free. Release him in your heart and mind and he will return to you.

Try – through prayer, meditation and making the mind still – to develop that communion of the heart I spoke of earlier. In this way you will be able to raise your consciousness to attune yourself to the level of awareness where you can link mentally with your child. If you can reach this state, you will not need a medium to tell you that he still lives. You will know, in your innermost being, that you are united, soul to soul.

Opening the Heart

Mick and Jo lost two children. A miscarriage cost Jo her daughter, Margaret. The following year, their two-year-old son Jason died under anaesthetic during an operation for a respiratory infection. Mick told me, 'You can't help but be changed by something like this. Material things lose all their value. When Jason first died, I was very bitter but I learned to open my heart instead.'

Mick and Jo are now both healers. They believe that they can do this work more effectively because what they have been through gives them a greater empathy with their patients. Over the years I have known many parents like them, who have come through their pain and are now helping other people, in many different ways. Some of them are healers and counsellors. A few are mediums, bringing other bereaved parents the comfort they have found themselves.

What helped them to avoid becoming locked in bitterness was the fact that they knew their children were living on in the spirit world. For all of them, I am sure, an ache remains that never goes away. But, in seeking spiritual contact with their children, they have found their own spirit within. This has given them strength and led them to explore the spiritual gifts that lay hidden within them, which they might otherwise never have discovered. And it is their children who, from the spirit world, have led them forward, giving them courage and inspiration.

No Separation

Even after the worst pain, the ability to feel joy can return. The spirit that is within us links us with all life, with our children and those we love in the spirit world and with God, the Universal Spirit, whatever you wish to call Him, in whose keeping no soul is ever lost.

The Rev. Carol E. Parrish-Harra, an American pastor, wrote *The New Age Handbook on Death and Dying*, based on her ministry to the terminally ill. Ironically, just as she had completed the book, she was called upon to face a traumatic loss in her own life, when her daughter and grand-daughter were killed in a car crash. At the end of her book, she wrote:

> As I try to think of my world without Mary Beth
> and the baby, I am acutely aware of the hole blown in
> the fabric of my existence; aware of the abrupt
> rupturing of my picture of her future and of my part
> interwoven into that future. Hopes explode in midair
> and plans jettison.
>
> The wise level of self puts in a word or two,
> interjects great wisdom which my mother/
> grandmother personality doesn't want to hear.
> Mother/grandmother wants to say, 'I can protect
> them. I deny this – I won't have it! Turn back the
> frames and let's replay this part of the movie. I
> demand a different script. This can't be so!'
>
> The wise and knowing part, vastly in tune with life,
> brings its wisdom to mother/grandmother and says,
> 'This is the stuff character is made of. You are a child
> of the Universe and you will experience what the
> Universe has to offer!'
>
> Once life is conceived, its entire rhythm is to be
> experienced. Breathe deeply; learn to flow with it.
> The great pain of your labour will be followed by the
> incredible beauty and joy of new life.
>
> The age old wisdom comes to us from every
> direction. Yesterday I buried my daughter and
> grandchild. Happily, today a man tells me of the
> birth of a new child and I smile at him with love. He
> has thus assured me of the continuity of life. Yes, it is
> security at its most basic level. My pain didn't stop
> all life. Thank God life is so huge; happiness and
> beauty are still out there taking place. I need that

reassurance. Now I can cry the mote from my eye, knowing that Beauty lives, knowing I *need* happy moments.

Happiness and beauty are still there, for us in this world and even more for those who have passed into the world beyond. So I would say to all bereaved parents: remember that your child in the spirit world is still part of your family, as much as your children on earth. Cry for them if you need to but be glad for them also and live for them – live in a way that will make them proud of you. They are part of you and you are part of them and where there is love, there can be no separation.

Useful Addresses

College of Psychic Studies, 16 Queensberry Place, London SW7 2EB. Private consultations with mediums, lectures, etc.

The Compassionate Friends, 6 Denmark Street, Clifton, Bristol, BS1 5DQ. Support group for bereaved parents. Many local branches.

Greater World Christian Spiritualist Association, 3–5 Conway Street, London W1P 5HA. Private consultations with mediums, lectures, etc.

Psychic World, 22 Kingsley Avenue, Southall, Middlesex UB1 2NA.

Roadpeace, PO Box 2570, London NW10 3PW. Support groups for families who have suffered bereavement through road death.

SANDS, 28 Portland Place, London, W1N 3DE. Stillbirth and Neonatal Death Society.

SIBSS, PO Box 295, York, YO2 5YP. Support group for bereaved brothers and sisters.

SOS (Shadow of Suicide) c/o The Compassionate Friends, 6 Denmark Street, Clifton, Bristol BS1 5DQ.

Spiritualist Association of Great Britain, 33 Belgrave Square, London SW1X 8QB. Private consultations with mediums, lectures, etc.

Spiritualists National Union, Stansted Hall, Stansted, Essex CM24 8UD. Residental courses, lectures, demonstrations.

Overseas

American Federation of Spiritualist Churches Inc., 145 Herring Pond Road, Buzzards Bay, MA 02532, USA.

Centre of Spiritual Studies, PO Box 12234, Centrahil, 6006, Port Elizabeth, R. South Africa.

Greater World Christian Spiritualist Association, 3–5 Conway Street, London W1P 5HA, UK. The association has affiliated churches throughout the UK, Northern Ireland, Channel Islands, Australia, Canada, Nigeria and South Africa.

National Spiritualists' Association Churches, c/o Rev. S.L. Snowman, PO Box 217, Lily Dale, New York 14752, USA.

Spiritualist Alliance (Auckland) Inc., PO Box 9477, 120 Carlton Gore Road, Newmarket, Auckland 1, New Zealand.

BIBLIOGRAPHY AND RECOMMENDED READING

Sylvia Barbanell, *When a Child Dies* (1942, Psychic Press)

M'Haletta & Carmella B'Hahn, *Benjaya's Gifts* (1996, Hazelwood Press, Loddiswell, Nr. Kingsbridge, Devon TQ7 4EB)

Gwen Byrne, *Russell* (1994, Janus Publishing Co.)

Colin Caffell, *In Search of the Rainbow's End* (1994, Hodder and Stoughton)

Peter Cowlin, *Listen Who Dares* (1994, Suilvern Publishing. Available from L.N. Fowler, 1201 High Road, Chadwell Heath, Romford, Essex RM6 4DH)

Peter Cowlin, *Truth is Veiled* (1991, Synthesis Publishing, Available from L.N. Fowler)

Olivia Cox, *Sunday's Child* (1988, Ashgrove Press Ltd)

Jane Davies, *The Price of Loving* (1986, Mowbray)

Peter Fenwick, *The Truth in the Light* (1995, Headline)

Kate Hill, *The Long Sleep* (1995, Virago Press)

Elisabeth Kübler-Ross, *On Children and Death* (1983, Collier Books, USA)

Harold S. Kushner, *When Bad Things Happen to Good People* (1981, Pan Books)

Georgiana Monckton, *Dear Isobel* (1994, Vermilion)

Raymond Moody, *The Light Beyond* (1988, Bantam Books)

Melvin Morse, *Closer to the Light* (1990, Bantam Books)

Melvin Morse, *Parting Visions* (1994, Piatkus Books)

Stephen O'Brien, *Voices From Heaven* (1991, Harper Collins)

Carol E. Parrish-Harra, *The New Age Handbook on Death and Dying* (1989, Sparrowhawk Press, USA)

Jasper Swain, *On the Death of My Son* (1974, Turnstone Press)

Marilyn Shaw (ed), *Enduring, Sharing, Loving* (1992, Darton Longman and Todd Ltd. In association with the Alder Centre, Royal Liverpool Children's Hospital, Alder Hey, Eaton Road, Liverpool L12 2AP)

Cherie Sutherland, *Children of the Light* (1995, Souvenir Press)

Iris Thomas, *Thy Son Lives* (1997, Homere Publishing, Clock House, Stansted Hall, Stansted, Essex CM24 8UD)

Linda Williamson, *Contacting the Spirit World* (1996, Piatkus Books)

Linda Williamson, *Mediums and the Afterlife* (1992, Robert Hale)

Linda Williamson, *Mediums and their Work* (1990, Robert Hale)

INDEX

Also by Linda Williamson

CONTACTING THE SPIRIT WORLD
*How to develop your psychic abilities and stay
in touch with loved ones*

When a loved one dies, it is natural to want to find out what
has happened to them. Have they ceased to exist or are they
living in another world? What kind of world is it? Is it possible to get in touch? Is the feeling of their continuing presence real or just your imagination? In *Contacting the Spirit
World*, experienced medium Linda Williamson provides
many of the answers and shows you how to develop your
own powers as a medium.

Linda Williamson draws on her own experiences and
those of other mediums and sitters to offer inspiration and
encouragement to those wishing to develop their psychic
abilities and to give comfort to the bereaved. Practical and
enlightening, *Contacting the Spirit World* will open your eyes
to the world of life after death.

Available from Piatkus at £8.99 (pbk)
ISBN: 0 7499 1596 X